# 30-SECOND
# BEER

# 30-SECOND
# BEER

The 50 essential elements of producing
and enjoying the world's beers, each
explained in half a minute

Editor
**Sophie Atherton**

Foreword
**Roger Ryman**

Contributors
**Sophie Atherton**
**Jerry Bartlett**
**Pete Brown**
**Jeff Evans**
**Susanna Forbes**
**Roger Protz**

Illustrations
**Nicky Ackland-Snow**

**IVY PRESS**

First published in the UK in 2018 by
**Ivy Press**
An imprint of The Quarto Group
The Old Brewery, 6 Blundell Street
London N7 9BH, United Kingdom
**T** (0)20 7700 6700 **F** (0)20 7700 8066
www.QuartoKnows.com

British Library Cataloguing-in-
Publication Data
A catalogue record for this
book is available from the
British Library.

ISBN: 978-1-78240-548-1

This book was conceived,
designed and produced by
**Ivy Press**
58 West Street, Brighton BN1 2RA, UK

Publisher **Susan Kelly**
Creative Director **Michael Whitehead**
Editorial Director **Tom Kitch**
Commissioning Editor **Sophie Collins**
Project Editor **Caroline Earle**
Designer **Ginny Zeal**
Picture researcher **Sharon Dortenzio**
Glossaries **Jerry Bartlett**

Printed in China

10 9 8 7 6 5 4 3 2 1

# CONTENTS

# FOREWORD
Roger Ryman

I have been working in the beer industry for almost 30 years. As the brewing director of two West Country breweries (St Austell Brewery and Bath Ales) I've overseen the expansion and modernization of both brew houses and developed recipes for some of the best-selling cask ales in the UK. I've also been fortunate enough to have travelled and gained inspiration from countries around the world, sourcing the very best ingredients and tasting the greatest beers. Ultimately I'm a beer drinker, a beer enthusiast and feel lucky to be paid to do what I love for a living.

Having been part of the vibrant British brewing scene since the late twentieth century, it's been astonishing to see how beer culture has evolved. It has progressed further in the past decade than at any other time and shows no sign of slowing down, as the desire for top-quality and flavoursome options continues to grow. There's no better time to be a beer drinker.

In one form or another, grain-fermented liquids have been a staple part of life around the world, for thousands of years. Beer is the oldest recorded recipe in the world. I therefore salute this group of writers who have collaborated to condense the history of beer into one essential guide. Those who have contributed are diverse in their areas of expertise and experience but have two things in common – their depth of knowledge and their love of beer.

Interest in understanding more about the origins of beer, and how best to enjoy it, has never been more prevalent, therefore the timing of *30-Second Beer* couldn't be better. It's succinct and educational enough for those who are new to beer and the perfect reference guide for well-informed aficionados.

# INTRODUCTION
Sophie Atherton

Humans have been brewing and drinking beer for millennia, but the last couple of decades can be seen as one of the most – if not *the* most – exciting periods to be a beer drinker. Immediately beforehand, the choice was between cold, yellow, fizzy lager or not-so-fizzy brown beer, which in the UK largely meant cask ale. Cask ale packed more flavour, but for many it still wasn't much to choose from. In some places lager was the only option – sometimes it still is. But there is an incredible new world of beer beyond it, awash with an amazing variety of delicious drinks to choose from. This is the wonder of beer. Although the craft brewing revolution has successfully added all manner of fruits, spices and plants (such as tea, coffee and chocolate) to beer, it is still most often made from just four ingredients: malted barley, water, yeast and hops. Within those four ingredients exists such diversity and variety that by careful selection, and adjusting techniques and recipes accordingly, brewers can produce hundreds of different types of beer – each with its own unique flavour. The range of alcoholic strengths, from virtually zero to as strong as spirits, is also astonishing. There truly is a beer for everyone; all tastes are catered for.

The excitement has been infectious. All around the world numbers of breweries have increased. Global corporations still do their best to dominate, but more and more places now have a small, local brewer. Interest in these artisanal craft beer producers remains strong, even in the face of decreasing beer sales. Drinking less but better is a big part of the craft beer philosophy, which is why understanding more about what you're drinking is definitely an advantage.

### How the book works
In the following pages, I and five fellow beer writers walk you through the beer world. We all adore beer and during our respective careers have amassed a sizeable amount of knowledge about it. We can't share all of it here, but we'll give you the best introduction we can, to enjoying

beer as much as we do. The seven chapters attempt to package beer into drinkable measures – because we don't want to get you drunk. **The Basics** is the beery foundation upon which the book sits. It shows where beer originally came from, clears up the beer versus lager conundrum, demonstrates that beer isn't just something 'chugged' in pints and offers explanation of why some beer is fizzier than others. In **History**, we flesh out these topics, looking a little more closely at the origins of beer, some of its key players and significant historic periods. Next comes **Brewing**, where we tell you how beer is made and from what. Then we look at different types of beer, or **Beer Styles**. This chapter is a mixture of history, detail of how beer's ingredients produce different results and what they taste like. **Beer Culture** is a round-the-world trip visiting major brewing nations and locations – looking at where beer has come from and how it's developed depending on where it's brewed. **The Beer Industry** looks at how beer is sold to us and influences on the trade. We saved the best till last. **Beer Appreciation** aims to demonstrate the value of understanding what you're tasting; how to spot the worst and get the best from beer; considers tasting opportunities and introduces a cast of characters who judge, write about and campaign for beer.

For each of the topics, the 3-Second Taster gives an instant overview, the 30-Second Beer tells you the detail and the 3-Minute Brew offers extra information to whet your appetite for finding out more – either by reading or tasting. Whether you are new to beer, rediscovering it, or just reminding yourself of the hows, whys and wheres, we hope that you'll enjoy this book, preferably with a glass of delicious beer close to hand.

# THE BASICS

**alcohol by volume**  Measure of the alcoholic strength of a beer. The percentage of the volume of the beer that is pure alcohol, usually abbreviated to % ABV.

**bottle shop**  A retail establishment specializing in a wide range of beers predominantly for consumption off the premises. In modern usage, often used to differentiate from a shop or store where more widely marketed and non-artisanal alcoholic beverages can be bought.

**cask** (n.)  A container for beer to be served in a bar or pub which holds cask ale. Casks are used for maturing (and conditioning) unfiltered, unpasteurized beer – cask ale (often called real ale). When the beer in a cask is served, it is not dispensed using carbon dioxide. (adj.) Denoting beer dispensed from or matured in a cask.

**cellaring**  The crafts and skills associated with keeping beer at good quality for serving in a pub or bar. Especially associated with the skills required to keep and serve cask ale in UK pubs so that it reaches the customer in peak condition. Also referred to as 'cellarmanship'.

**conditioning**  The final stage in the process of maturing beer to prepare it for drinking. If unfiltered and unpasteurized, the beer continues to ferment slowly, and the carbon dioxide produced provides a fizz (carbonation), also called condition. Beer may also be force-carbonated to achieve the required level of carbonation.

**degrees Plato**  An indicator of the eventual strength of a finished beer, it is a measure of the density of the wort, and therefore indicates the amount of sugars present before they are fermented into alcohol. Degrees Plato are converted to percentage alcohol by volume (ABV) by calculating 0.4% ABV for every 1°. Roughly equivalent to degrees Balling.

**flavour profile**  Description of the taste of beer, usually including its perceived bitterness, sweetness or dryness, acidity, and so on, and often including a description of aromas and other flavour components.

**force carbonating**  A method of adding carbon dioxide to a beer. While under pressure (in keg or bottle) the carbon dioxide remains in solution, emerging as bubbles when the beer is served. Most often used on beers that have been pasteurized or when a beer does not contain the required level of carbonation.

**keg** (n.) A container for beer to be served in a bar, usually made of aluminium, but sometimes plastic. The beer in a keg is usually pressurized with and dispensed by carbon dioxide, sometimes mixed with nitrogen. (adj.) Denoting beer dispensed from a keg.

**KeyKeg®** A type of keg in which the beer is held in an inner plastic bag and is dispensed by a propellant gas squeezing the bag rather than coming into direct contact with the beer.

**mouthfeel** The physical sensation of beer in the taster's mouth. The subjective appreciation of the texture of a beer on the tongue and palate.

**original gravity** Measure of the density of a beer before it is fermented, compared to water, indicating its likely alcoholic strength after fermentation. For example, a beer's original gravity might be measured as 1045 OG, which, because water is 1000 OG, shows about how much sugar there is to be fermented (the excess is not all sugars).

**Trappist** Denoting beers brewed at a Trappist monastery recognized by the International Trappist Association. Trappist beers are often strong (7–10% ABV) and usually conform to styles originating in Belgium. Beers brewed in similar styles but not at one of these monasteries are known as Abbey-style beers.

**wort** The sugary liquid that results from the mashing process, in which, in the simplest case, the milled grains are soaked in water at about 67°C (153°F) for 90 minutes or so and then drained.

# WHAT IS BEER?

## the 30-second beer

**3-SECOND TASTER**
Beer is a complex, fermented drink that embodies the taste, flavour, culture and style of every society that crafts it.

**3-MINUTE BREW**
Since its discovery in ancient times, beer has been inextricably linked to the economy. Ancient Egypt had its Royal Chief Beer Inspectors, and workers building the pyramids were part paid in beer. From Babylonian times, strict rules have recognized beer's importance, in many cases enforcing quality and regulating prices. Today, the number of breweries worldwide continues to rise. In the USA alone, the beer industry as a whole generates over $250 billion, employing 1.75 million people.

Beer is for everyone; from presidents in palaces to men and women in street bars and country fields. Discovered over 5,000 years ago, today it's brewed everywhere, from Albania to Zambia, each country developing its own brewing identity and beer traditions. The simplest definition of beer is of an alcoholic drink produced when malted cereal, generally barley, is fermented using yeast. Hops are added for their aromatic, bittering and preservative properties. After water and tea, beer is the world's third most popular drink. Long recognized for its intoxicating powers, for centuries beer was healthier than water. The progress of beer follows the advances of technology, as seen with the emergence of light-coloured malts and the rise of pale ale in the nineteenth century. What sets beer apart is its sheer array of flavours, textures and aromas. The Babylonians defined 20 styles of beer, and today there are hundreds, from a fragrant, quaffable pilsner through to an exotically complex imperial stout. Beer's ability to encompass a wide range of alcoholic strengths also makes it remarkably versatile. The perfect dining companion, pub and bar cultures have grown up around the world to serve and look after beer, and now specialist bottle shops offer the home drinker the same chance to enjoy and experiment.

**RELATED ENTRIES**
See also
THE ORIGINS OF BEER
page 30

SAFER THAN WATER
page 34

HOW BEER IS MADE
page 48

**3-SECOND BIOGRAPHY**
NINKASI
**fl. c. 1800 BCE**
Leading goddess in ancient Sumeria, whose remit included beer and brewing; she inspired poems giving the earliest description of how beer is brewed

**30-SECOND TEXT**
Susanna Forbes

*Everyone drank beer in ancient Egypt, from lowly workers to high-ranking pharaohs, making the growing of grain a fundamental part of the economy.*

# ALE VERSUS LAGER

## the 30-second beer

There are two distinct definitions of ale and lager in popular use. They're closely related, but quite different. The first revolves around the process of conditioning after the main fermentation, a process whereby the flavours round out and knit together. Broadly speaking, ales condition for a few days and are then ready to drink quickly, while lagers prefer a slow, cool conditioning process of at least 30 days, ideally more. This process gives lager its name – the word is German for 'to store'. But ales can be 'lagered', or stored, too, and most commercial 'lagers' are not lagered at all. So the second distinction is the most useful one, and it is that ale yeasts and lager yeasts are genetically different families that behave in different ways during the main fermentation process. Ale yeast ferments quickly at warmer temperatures, tends to give the beer a fruitier character, often referred to as being 'estery', and rises to the top of the vessel during fermentation. Lager yeasts ferment slowly at cooler temperatures and give less contribution to flavour, leaving a cleaner, crisper drink. They sink to the bottom of the vessel after fermenting. Hence ale and lager yeasts are often referred to as 'top-fermenting' and 'bottom-fermenting' respectively.

**RELATED ENTRIES**
See also
FERMENTATION
page 50

YEAST
page 60

**3-SECOND TASTER**
Ale and lager are beer's two main families, and the difference between them is not necessarily colour, flavour or temperature but the yeasts that ferment them.

**3-MINUTE BREW**
*Saccharomyces cerevisiae* is the name of the traditional yeast that ferments ale, as well as wine and bread. Lager yeast – commonly known as *Saccharomyces pastorianus* – is a genetic hybrid of *S. cerevisiae* and another yeast called *S. eubayanus*. The origins of *S. eubayanus* have been conclusively traced to South American forests. But lager yeast has been present in central Europe since well before European ships brought goods back from the New World. No one has yet figured out how it got here.

**3-SECOND BIOGRAPHY**
EMIL CHRISTIAN HANSEN
1842–1909
Danish scientist who built on Louis Pasteur's work on the link between yeast and fermentation; Hansen successfully isolated single yeast cells, allowing them to be cultivated in laboratory conditions that ensured consistency and reliability, creating the first commercial lager yeast

**30-SECOND TEXT**
Pete Brown

*Ale and lager are largely defined by how their differing yeasts behave in the brewing process.*

# ALCOHOLIC STRENGTH

## the 30-second beer

**3-SECOND TASTER**
The strength of a beer is determined by how much fermentable sugar is turned into alcohol and there are various ways of measuring this.

**3-MINUTE BREW**
Brewer's yeast usually stops working at around 11% ABV, unable to tolerate the alcohol it has created, and so a wine yeast is often then employed to take beer to higher strengths. Some brewers freeze distil their beer to increase strength. Water freezes at a higher temperature than alcohol, so this process creates ice crystals in the liquid that can then be removed, increasing the concentration of alcohol.

Numerous methods of indicating alcoholic strength have been employed over the years, some based on the amount of sugar in the wort (the liquid produced by mashing) before it is fermented. These include systems known as degrees Plato and degrees Balling, which calculate the weight of the sugar as a percentage of the entire wort, and the original gravity system (OG) that reflects the overall density of the wort compared to water. Both offer only a rough guide to the actual strength of a beer because strength is ultimately decided by the length and efficiency of the fermentation process. More accurate methods therefore refer to the percentage of alcohol in the finished liquid. The alcohol by weight percentage (ABW) was once prevalent in the USA but globally accepted as the norm today is alcohol by volume (ABV). In terms of the definition of beer, there is no upper limit for alcoholic strength. While the vast majority of beers fall comfortably below the 10% ABV level, there are some that rocket into areas normally only occupied by fortified wines and spirits. Personal preference obviously dictates the favoured strength but the most successful brewers ensure that strength is not the be-all and end-all. If alcohol is out of balance with the body and flavours of a beer, it can taste crude, hot and unpleasant.

**RELATED ENTRIES**
See also
WHAT IS BEER?
page 16

HOW BEER IS MADE
page 48

FERMENTATION
page 50

YEAST
page 60

**3-SECOND BIOGRAPHY**
ROBERT BOYLE
1627–91
Inventor of the hydrometer, the instrument that allows brewers to measure the amount of sugar in their worts

**30-SECOND TEXT**
Jeff Evans

*Beer comes in a range of alcoholic strengths, which are normally expressed as the ABV 'alcohol by volume'.*

**747 CE**
An abbey is built at St Gallen in what is today Switzerland. Architectural drawings from the ninth century show a brewhouse and bakery

**11th century**
Monks are brewing at both Weltenburg and Weihenstephan monasteries in Bavaria

**Late 18th century**
Monks at La Trappe in Normandy are driven from France by the revolution and settle in the Low Countries

**1793**
French Revolutionaries sack the abbey of Orval, believing Louis XV was hiding there. Abbey and brewery are rebuilt in the twentieth century

**1794**
Monks granted land at Westmalle near Antwerp start to build an abbey, completed in 1804

**1831**
Monks found the Westvleteren abbey near Ypres

**1850**
17 monks from Westvleteren are given permission to leave and build a new abbey on land granted by the Prince of Chimay

**1887**
Monks rebuild the abbey at Rochefort, abandoned during the French Revolution, adding a brewery two years later

**1932**
The Abbot of Westmalle, Edmond Ooms, labels his beers 'Trappisten beer' and the other abbeys follow suit

**1998**
Monks at Achel restore brewing at an abbey founded in 1845: the brewery was wrecked during the First World War. They are helped in restoring brewing by brothers from Westmalle

**2013**
St Joseph's Abbey, Massachusetts becomes the first certified Trappist brewery in the USA – and the first outside Europe. The brewery is named Spencer after the town where the monastery is located

**2018**
Mount St Bernard Abbey, Leicestershire, becomes the UK's first Trappist brewery as monks there begin making Tynt Meadow ale

# MONASTIC BREWERS

While a few monasteries still brew in Austria, Germany and the Netherlands, Belgium is the most celebrated country for beers brewed by monks. The abbeys keep alive a tradition stretching back to the ninth and eleventh centuries, when monks in Switzerland and Bavaria started to brew. Beer helped sustain the monks, who had frugal diets. They called beer 'liquid bread' and it was especially important during the Lenten fast. The knowledge of brewing was spread both by pilgrims and monks as they travelled to and from Rome. The Church's grip was broken at the time of the Reformation. But brewing has survived in Belgium, where six Trappist abbeys produce beers that have become famous throughout the world for their depth of flavour and character.

The monks are members of the Cistercian Order of the Strict Observance. They were based at La Trappe in Normandy, from which they derive the name Trappists. Driven out of France during the French Revolution in the late eighteenth century, they settled in the Low Countries. They were granted land and built small chapels that grew into substantial abbeys over the years. One abbey, at Orval, is older and was built by Benedictines in the eleventh century; it was later rebuilt by the Trappists.

In France the monks had made liqueurs, which helps explain the strength of Trappist beers – many are as strong as wine.

In the twentieth century, the monks started to sell small amounts of beer commercially. During both world wars, invading German troops stripped the breweries of their copper vessels, and the monks needed investment to rebuild them and also to develop their missionary work. At Chimay, the head brewer, Father Théodore, consulted brewing scientists at Leuven University to design a modern brewhouse and to develop new styles of beer. Sales grew in the late twentieth century when beer writers, notably the late Michael Jackson, wrote favourably about the beers, and demand from abroad led to increased production.

The six Trappist breweries in Belgium are Achel, Chimay, Orval, Rochefort, Westmalle and Westvleteren. Beers brewed here, or in other Trappist monasteries elsewhere, carry a seal from the Trappist Association. This protects the integrity of the beers and distinguishes them from commercial abbey-style brews. There may be no 'Trappist style' (each monastery makes its own distinctive versions), but Belgian Trappist brews are so popular they are exported worldwide and also inspire secular brewers on both sides of the Atlantic.

*Roger Protz*

# PACKAGING & DISPENSE

## the 30-second beer

### 3-SECOND TASTER

Traditionalists say kegs make beer too fizzy, but modern brewers say higher carbonation suits some beer styles – even cans are good, these days.

### 3-MINUTE BREW

Arguably, the reason this topic and the modern beer world exist is because of UK pressure group CAMRA, which champions cask beer. But as casks require careful cellaring, their use in other countries has been limited. Single-use plastic kegs (such as KeyKeg®) hold the beer in a polythene bag. Pressure on the bag – not in the keg – dispenses the beer. Plastic kegs can be used for any style that doesn't need force carbonating – even 'cask' ales.

The package your beer comes in and how it gets to the glass is the subject of fierce debate: keg versus cask, can versus bottle. Casks, championed by The Campaign for Real Ale (CAMRA), are used mostly for British beer styles. CAMRA says beer from casks must be unpasteurized, and crucially, cannot use artificially introduced gas in contact with beer to dispense or carbonate it. Otherwise it's not real ale. Unlike casks, kegs are completely sealed and use gas pressure to dispense the beer. Done well, traditional cask ale is beautifully nuanced and flavourful. Traditionalists say, 'If we allow kegs, soon we'll all be drinking flavourless fizz out of cans.' 'Ah,' say modern keggers. 'Beer styles like American IPAs, imperial porters and pilsners benefit from the higher carbonation that kegs allow, plus they keep fresher for longer.' They add, 'There's nothing wrong with cans, either.' Beer in kegs and cans can (now) also be unfiltered and unpasteurized – just as 'real' as cask ale. Modern brewing techniques have created new beer styles and refreshed old ones. Improved technology and materials deliver flavour and mouthfeel without metallic or plastic taint. Cans exclude light that ruins hop flavour and are more environmentally friendly. Surely, the best method to serve beer is what best serves the type of beer. Or, just as you like it.

### RELATED ENTRIES

See also
BEER IN THE TWENTIETH CENTURY
page 42

BEER CHAMPIONS
page 152

### 3-SECOND BIOGRAPHIES

**BERT HANSSEN**
1966–
Dutch inventor of the KeyKeg® and the technical director of Lightweight Containers, the company that promotes and sells them

**DALE KATECHIS**
1969–
Founder of Oskar Blues Brewery, Colorado in 1997. In 2002, it became the first American craft brewery to can its own beer

### 30-SECOND TEXT

Jerry Bartlett

*New packaging technology alongside traditional methods helps your beer reach you as the brewer would want.*

# HISTORY

**alpha acids** Resinous components of hops that, during the boiling stage in the brewing process, add bitterness to balance the natural sweetness of the beer. The percentage of alpha acids in different varieties of hops is a measure of the bittering potential of the hop variety, or batch.

**Bohemia** A historic region of central Europe, now forming the western part of the Czech Republic.

**cask ale** Ale that has been matured and conditioned in a cask without having been pasteurized and with little or no filtration. As live yeast remains, the beer continues to ferment slowly, providing a light, natural carbonation when the beer is served. It is not dispensed using carbon dioxide $(CO_2)$, as is the case with other draught beer, but drawn through pipes running from pub cellar to bar, by means of a piston pump system. It may also be served using a tap inserted directly into the cask. Often also called real ale.

**cold fermentation** Fermentation using yeast adapted to working at temperatures of around 7–13°C (45–55°F), compared to 17–22°C (62–72°F) for warm fermentation. Cold fermentation yeasts tend to sink, so the process is often called bottom fermentation. Warm fermentation yeasts tend to produce a foamy cap of yeast, hence 'top fermentation'. Cold-fermented beers (generally lagers) are often less fruitily aromatic compared to warm-fermented beers.

**craft brewery** Essentially, an independent brewery, typically a small one that is wholly or largely independently owned, and often (but not always or exclusively) producing beer styles influenced by modern American breweries. In the USA, the Brewers Association defines a craft brewer as 'small, independent and traditional'. It stipulates maximum levels of annual production and no more than 25% ownership or control by an individual or business that is not itself a craft brewer. There is no formal definition outside the USA and this has been a source of contention, especially in the UK.

**enzyme** A type of naturally occurring protein that acts as a catalyst, driving and accelerating chemical reactions. In beer making, Enzymes present in barley are activated in the mashing process, where, in the presence of water at about 67°C (153°F), they convert unfermentable starches into fermentable sugars.

**hybrid beer** A beer made with a combination of fermentation methods and/or ingredients, such as used for both lagers and ale types, showing characteristics of more than one style of beer.

**Industrial Revolution** The rapid development of industry that began in Britain in the late eighteenth century, brought about by the introduction of machinery.

**IPA** Stands for India Pale Ale; a stronger version of the pale ale style.

**keg beer** Beer dispensed from a keg, characterized by using carbon dioxide or nitrogen pressure to force the beer out of its container. Typically, keg beers are served cooler and are more carbonated (fizzy) than cask beer. Keg beer is far more common than cask beer.

**pump clip** A small removable label, usually of plastic, wood or metal, attached to a beer-dispensing tap in a pub or bar; it identifies the beer being served, and usually the brewery. Pump clips are an important part of the brand identity. The name, in the UK at least, originates from its use on the handpump handles used to dispense cask ale.

**Trappist** Denoting beers brewed at a Trappist monastery recognized by the International Trappist Association. Trappist beers are often strong (7–10% ABV) and usually conform to styles originating in Belgium. Beers brewed in similar styles but not at one of these monasteries are known as Abbey-style beers.

# THE ORIGINS OF BEER

## the 30-second beer

Historians can't agree what came first: civilization or beer. Some say that nomadic tribes settled down specifically so they could set up agrarian systems to grow large quantities of grain and thus brew seriously. Others are not so sure. What they do agree on is that the malting process might have been triggered by wild grain being left out in the rain. Collected up and heated to make bread, the grain's starches would have begun the conversion to sugar. Add in a bit more rain plus wild yeasts, and fermentation could have taken place. Molecular archaeology traces beer back to the ancient Sumerians, over 5,000 years ago. Located in what is now Iraq, Sumeria is often called the cradle of civilization, being where nomads first put down roots. Beer swiftly became embedded into the culture, as it did with the Babylonian and Egyptian empires that followed. With their preference for wine, the Greeks and Romans were less enthused. As Catholicism took hold in much of Europe, the monasteries arrived, embracing brewing with fervour. From the start, beer's celebratory potential was well recognized along with its nutritional value. Alongside baking bread, brewing became the responsibility of women, which it remained until the Middle Ages. While the grains used might have varied, before 1000 CE the flavour came from herbs rather than hops.

**RELATED ENTRIES**
See also
MONASTIC BREWERS
page 22

WOMEN & BEER
page 32

SAFER THAN WATER
page 34

**3-SECOND BIOGRAPHY**
DR PATRICK E. MCGOVERN
1944–
Known as 'the Beer Archaeologist', Dr McGovern is the Scientific Director of the Biomolecular Archaeology Project for Cuisine, Fermented Beverages and Health at the University of Pennsylvania, Philadelphia; he recreated award-winning ancient beers with Sam Calagione at Dogfish Head Brewery, Delaware, USA

**30-SECOND TEXT**
Susanna Forbes

*For both its pleasurable and nutritional value, beer became an integral part of culture in the Sumerian, Babylonian and Egyptian empires.*

**3-SECOND TASTER**
First 'discovered' by the Sumerians over 5,000 years ago and for millennia often more hygienic to drink than water, beer's pleasurable and nutritious properties swiftly made it popular for all.

**3-MINUTE BREW**
The first beer laws arrived in Babylonian times. The famous Hammurabi Code not only defined 20 varieties of beer, but it also specified ration laws based on social standing and laid down purity and price regulations. From peasants to pharaohs, Egyptians embraced beer throughout society. Great grain stores were established and large breweries were built. Workers were paid with beer, taxes on beer were brought in and records speak of the 'beer of eternity' and 'garnished beer'.

# WOMEN & BEER

## the 30-second beer

### In the earliest brewing

civilizations, Sumeria, Babylon and Ancient Egypt, beer was made mostly by women. Fast forward a few thousand years and evidence from medieval England tells a similar story: brewing was women's work. They produced beer in the manner of a cottage industry, selling it from their homes or hawking it in the streets, but they were also brewing on a more commercial scale. Yet, in parallel with other historical examples of sex discrimination, as brewing became more profitable and industrialized, women were pushed out. There's also a correlation between women being expected to inhabit only the private space of the home, while men occupied public space – including the public house. It may not be the most important element in the battle for equality, but beer is a feminist issue. Not only was women's freedom to produce it curtailed, but public attitudes dictated they ought not to drink it either. Marketing, from advertising campaigns through to sexist beer names with pump clips to match, has done its best to promote the idea that beer is a man's drink. This is daft considering women make up half the population. Happily things are coming full circle. Growing numbers of women brewers, a glut of organizations representing women in the beer industry and increased interest among female drinkers show beer is a drink for all.

**RELATED ENTRY**
See also
THE ORIGINS OF BEER
page 30

**3-SECOND BIOGRAPHIES**
HILDEGARD VON BINGEN
1098–1179
Abbess of a Benedictine convent. She brewed beer and was probably the first person to write about hops in a scientific way. She also wrote about barley

SARA BARTON
1965–
Founder and head brewer of Brewster's Brewery, Lincolnshire. As well as naming her brewery after the term for female brewers, Sara's brewing ethos is to make beer appealing to all. She also brews a range of beers named after famous women

**30-SECOND TEXT**
Sophie Atherton

**3-SECOND TASTER**
Women were the first brewers and publicans – only in more recent times has beer been presented as being for men.

**3-MINUTE BREW**
In the 1970s Irish feminists staged a pub-based protest. Around 30 women each ordered a brandy, which they were served. They then asked for a pint of Guinness but were refused. They drank the brandy and left without paying. It was apparently legal to refuse to pay if there was an error with your order. Not allowing a woman her beer was clearly a grave error.

*Women's relationship with beer dates back thousands of years.*

# SAFER THAN WATER

## the 30-second beer

Beer has many attributes that make it appealing, but some of the most surprising are its health benefits. If you were living somewhere with unreliable water quality, beer could actually be safer to drink than water, for several reasons. First, alcohol itself is anti-bacterial – which is why it's used for swabbing in medicine. Second, the alpha acids in hops are also anti-bacterial, which allows beer to stay clean of harmful micro-organisms even at low alcohol strengths. And third, beer is boiled during its production, sterilizing the water in the brew. Because of all this, it's commonly asserted among brewing historians that beer was widely drunk because it was a safer alternative to drinking water. But the generality of this assertion has been questioned. Throughout history, supplies of drinkable water were not difficult for most people to obtain (outside of urban slums). Also, sterilization through boiling has long been understood – why not simply boil the water rather than go to the expense of brewing? The answer was likely the same then as it is now: people preferred beer because of its flavour, drinkability and 'buzz'. When life was so much harder, these attributes were even more important than they are today.

**RELATED ENTRIES**
See also
HOW BEER IS MADE
page 48

FERMENTATION
page 50

HOPS
page 54

WATER
page 62

**30-SECOND TEXT**
Pete Brown

**3-SECOND TASTER**
For most of our history beer has been safer to drink than water, but that's not necessarily the main reason our ancestors drank so much of it.

**3-MINUTE BREW**
Beer doesn't necessarily have to be boiled during production. It takes much more fuel and energy to boil water than it does to get to the warm temperature required for the enzymes in the malt to break down sugar ready for fermentation. It seems boiling only entered the picture when hops became the dominant flavouring in beer, around the fifteenth century – further undermining the theory that beer was an essential alternative to water.

*Because the brewing process includes boiling water, and – later – because of the antiseptic properties of hops, beer was considered a hygienic drink.*

# BEER & THE INDUSTRIAL REVOLUTION

## the 30-second beer

**3-SECOND TASTER**
Before the technological advances of the Industrial Revolution, all beer was dark and summer brewing turned beer sour.

**3-MINUTE BREW**
You can enjoy dark lagers in Germany and the Czech Republic but most lager beers today are pale gold and account for around 90% of all beer brewed worldwide. In spite of the popularity of lager, brewers in Britain and Ireland remained faithful to ale, including stout. Ale is made with a different type of 'top-fermenting' yeast that creates rich, fruity aromas and flavours. Today, with the popularity of IPA, ale is enjoying greater appreciation.

**It's hard to believe in an age** of pale ales and golden lagers, but until the Industrial Revolution *all* beers were brown. Malt was kilned or heated over smoky wood fires and the result was brown malt. When coke replaced wood it was possible to produce much paler malt with a higher level of enzymes in the grain that turn starch into fermentable sugar. The result was pale ale and stronger India Pale Ale (IPA) in England. European brewers rushed to England to see how pale ale was made then returned home to fashion pale lager. The major breakthrough was in Bohemia – now the Czech Republic – where the first golden lager was brewed in Pilsen. It was called Pilsner Urquell or Original Pilsner and it took the world by storm. Brewing for centuries had been seasonal and couldn't take place in summer as high temperatures turned beer sour. Production was transformed in the nineteenth century by ice-making machines and refrigeration that allowed beer to be stored in cool cellars. In the Carlsberg laboratories in Copenhagen, a scientist called Emil Hansen isolated a pure strain of 'bottom-fermenting' yeast that enabled beer to be brewed that was both clear and free from infection. Carlsberg allowed other brewers to use its yeast and lager beer went on to conquer the world.

**RELATED ENTRIES**
See also
ALE VERSUS LAGER
page 18

JOSEF GROLL
page 38

**3-SECOND BIOGRAPHY**
MARTIN STELZER
1815–94
Founder of the Burghers' Brewery in Pilsen; he recruited brewer Josef Groll who would go on to become the father of modern lager

**30-SECOND TEXT**
Roger Protz

*The technical progress brought about by the Industrial Revolution is responsible for the golden beers we know today.*

**21 August 1813**
Born in Vilshofen an der
Donau, Bavaria

**1838**
Dissatisfied beer drinkers
in Bohemian city of Plzen
(Pilsen, Czech Republic)
destroy 36 casks of beer
in the streets, citing poor
beer quality

**1839**
Martin Stelzer recruits
Groll for a new brewery
in Pilsen, Bürgerbrauerei
(Burghers' Brewery)

**5 October 1842**
Brews the first batch
of the pale golden lager
that became known as
Pilsner Urquell

**11 November 1842**
The pubs Zum Goldenen
Anker, Zur Weißen Rose
and Hanes in Pilsen
serve the new beer for
the first time

**30 April 1845**
Groll's contract at
Bürgerbrauerei expires;
he returns to Bavaria
and eventually inherits
his father's brewery
in Vilshofen

**1859**
Bürgerbrauerei registers
'Pilsner Bier' as a
trademark well after
imitators of the style
had begun to market
pilsner-style beers

**22 November 1887**
Dies in Vilshofen, but
not, as legend has it,
at his local

**1898**
Bürgerbrauerei registers
the trademark Pilsner
Urquell/Plzeňský
Prazdroj (German/Czech),
roughly, 'Pilsner from
the original source'

**1899**
Bürgerbrauerei loses
injunction sought in
1898 against the
Thomass Brewery in
Munich, for producing
a blond lager called
Thomass PilsnerBier

# JOSEF GROLL

## Josef Groll was a Bavarian

brewer who invented pilsner lager, the style of beer that gave rise to about 95% of the beer consumed in the world today. Remarkably, very few people have heard of him. Groll was already a highly regarded brewer in his hometown of Vilshofen, Bavaria, when he was recruited by a Bohemian start-up brewery, Bürgerbrauerei (Burghers' Brewery), Plzeň (Pilsen), in what is now the Czech Republic.

Legend has it that the beer-loving citizens of Pilsen, in an act of rebellion against the poor quality of beer in their town, smashed 36 casks of the offending beverage in the streets and demanded better. The new brewery was commissioned, and one of the designers, architect Martin Stelzer, as well as bringing new technologies to the venture, also recruited Josef Groll. It turned out to be a perfect set of circumstances. Groll, who was already skilled in the new Bavarian styles of cold-fermented beer, took advantage of the technology researched by Stelzer and the local ingredients. He used Bohemian malts, but pale versions, using techniques perfected for British pale ales, pure yeast strains, the soft local water and the aromatic local Saaz (Žatec) hops (although it is likely that other hops were used at first). With access to deep cellars for cool maturation (lagering) of the newly made beer, the result was a clear, golden, refreshing, aromatic beer. This new style of beer was an instant hit on its launch in Pilsen at the Martinmas celebrations of 1842.

What happened next seems to be a result of mismanagement, and unwillingness to deal with a man whose own father deemed him 'the rudest man in Bavaria'. When Groll's contract expired in 1845 it wasn't renewed and he returned to his father's brewery in Vilshofen, just across the border. The new beer style took off in the region and its reputation spread further through Bavaria and the rest of Europe, becoming known as pilsner (from Pilsen), or pilsener. However, no trademark on the style or name was registered until much later; the loss of an appellation-like control for the originator became a gain for the brewers of the world. Not even registering the trademark Pilsner Urquell (pilsner from the original source) helped.

Groll later took over his father's brewery and remained in his home town until his death in 1887. And although the beer style that he invented has spread worldwide, few know who the originator was.

*Jerry Bartlett*

# ORIGINS OF MODERN ALES

## the 30-second beer

### The Industrial Revolution

wrought two changes to brewing. First, it introduced new technologies that allowed brewers a much greater degree of quality control over their beers. Second, it allowed those who invested in brewing to benefit from economies of scale: the more beer they brewed, the cheaper it became. Brewing changed from an artisanal to an industrial activity, and that dramatically affected the style of beer brewed. Britain – the first industrialized country – was the first to experience this brewing revolution, and the first to develop new, industrial styles. The first industrial beer was porter, which was aged in wooden vats. The bigger the vats, the cheaper and more consistent the beer. Porter became hugely popular in London, brewed by new, industrial brewers such as Whitbread and Barclay Perkins. Arthur Guinness took the recipe home with him to Dublin, where his son, Arthur II, created a richer, 'extra stout' version that eventually became known simply as 'stout'. Coke smelting allowed greater control over malting barley, which allowed greater consistency in pale malt. Pale ales grew in popularity, particularly when exported to India, where they were perfect for the climate. By the 1820s, 'India Pale Ales', along with curry and silks, were the height of fashion in London, and pale ales began to rival and eventually overtake porter in popularity.

**3-SECOND TASTER**
Our most legendary ale styles have their roots in a similar time and place: London, in the heat of the Industrial Revolution, where beer met science and technology for the first time.

**3-MINUTE BREW**
Beer styles aren't created – they evolve. That's why there are no accurate dates or places for when they were first brewed, only times when they became commonly referred to by these names. Strong pales ales were being sold in India for at least a hundred years before the earliest known use of the term 'India Pale Ale' in press advertisements. IPA and porter are still evolving today, if anything, faster than ever.

**RELATED ENTRIES**
See also
MONASTIC BREWERS
page 22

BEER & THE INDUSTRIAL
REVOLUTION
page 36

PALE ALES
page 70

STOUT & PORTER
page 72

ARTHUR GUINNESS
page 78

GREAT BRITAIN
page 94

**3-SECOND BIOGRAPHY**
SAMUEL WHITBREAD
1720–96
Brewer and politician whose Chiswell Street brewery pioneered many modern industrial brewing techniques

**30-SECOND TEXT**
Pete Brown

*The changes brought about by the Industrial Revolution dramatically changed the beer world.*

# BEER IN THE TWENTIETH CENTURY

## the 30-second beer

## The twentieth century began

badly for beer. The deprivations of the First World War saw restrictions on malt supply, leading to weaker beers and the decline of stronger styles such as barley wines, old ales and strong stouts. In the USA, Prohibition's ban on the production and sale of alcohol led to the destruction of the American brewing industry. Elsewhere, mergers and acquisitions meant widescale rationalization, with hundreds of breweries closing. As brewing companies became bigger and more powerful, the way in which beer was produced and marketed also changed. In the UK, pasteurized, filtered and pressurized keg beer was promoted in place of cask ale, a move that led to the consumer fighting back, with the foundation of the Campaign for Real Ale (CAMRA) to push for the revival of traditional beer. Its success, in turn, was partly the inspiration for a new generation of craft breweries in the USA; their adventure and expertise went on to change the face of beer production internationally. In particular, their use of boldly flavoured American hops encouraged others to bring the hop more to the fore and encouraged hop breeders to deliver new varieties. Along with the rediscovery of forgotten beer styles and the creation of new hybrid styles, this has given beer new status as a connoisseur drink and resulted in thousands of new breweries opening around the world.

**RELATED ENTRIES**
See also
AMERICAN CRAFT BEERS
page 86

GREAT BRITAIN
page 94

UNITED STATES
page 104

**3-SECOND BIOGRAPHIES**
FRANKLIN D. ROOSEVELT
1882–1945
32nd President of the USA, who repealed Prohibition, reviving the US economy, reducing crime and bringing beer back to the people

JIMMY CARTER
1924–
39th President of the USA, who legalized the right to homebrew in 1978, a move that opened up the sector, providing a catalyst for the birth of craft brewing

**30-SECOND TEXT**
Jeff Evans

**3-SECOND TASTER**
After an initial severe decline, beer ended the twentieth century in good shape, ready to take the world by storm in the new millennium.

**3-MINUTE BREW**
The Campaign for Real Ale (CAMRA) was founded in 1971 by four friends appalled by the deteriorating quality of beer in the UK. Big breweries were removing traditional cask ales from pubs and replacing them with more profitable, but less flavoursome, keg beers. The four decided to take a stand and soon found there were thousands of like-minded people ready to join them. A powerful consumer movement was born.

*It was a challenging period for beer, but also the time when the seeds of future revolutions were sown.*

**BREWING** ◐

# BREWING
## GLOSSARY

**alpha acids**  Resinous components of hops that, during the boiling stage in the brewing process, add bitterness to balance the natural sweetness of the beer.

**bottle conditioned**  Beer that continues to ferment in its bottle owing to the presence of yeast. Must be stored upright and, unless a yeasty or hazy style, poured carefully so as not to disturb the sediment.

**brewpub**  A pub or bar containing brewing equipment of sufficient capacity to make beer for sale on the premises.

**carboy**  A glass or plastic cylindrical container often used in homebrewing for fermenting beer. Typical capacity is 5 imperial gallons (22.7 litres).

**enzyme**  A type of naturally occurring protein that acts as a catalyst, driving and accelerating chemical reactions. Enzymes present in barley are activated in the mashing process, where, in the presence of water at about 67°C (153°F), they convert unfermentable starches into fermentable sugars.

**ester**  A chemical compound produced in beer as a by-product of fermentation, especially of ales. In moderate quantities esters can be desirable because of the aromas they impart.

**farmhouse beer**  A family of ales originally from northern France and parts of Belgium, brewed as seasonal beers in farmhouses in the cooler months then stored to provide refreshment for farm workers in the summer.

**Gose**  A wheat beer flavoured with coriander and brewed using salt or salty water. Originating from the Leipzig area of Germany, its popularity has increased in recent years.

**gruit**  A blend of hedgerow herbs used to flavour and season ales before the use of hops became widespread.

**isinglass**  A substance extracted from the swim bladders of fish, it is used to speed up the clarification (fining) of beer, by causing yeast particles to clump together and settle at the bottom of the cask.

**keeping quality** An approximate measure of how well a beer can remain fresh and palatable. Beer can rapidly acquire undesirable flavours when subjected to light and temperatures above about 11°C (52°F).

**Lambic** Acidic-tasting (sour) wheat beers from the Brussels area of Belgium, fermented by wild yeasts and bacteria allowed to settle on the wort cooling in open vessels in a process known as spontaneous fermentation.

**lupulin** Resinous powder from the lupulin glands of a hop cone that contains the alpha acids and other flavour compounds used in brewing.

**Reinheitsgebot** German for 'purity decree', commonly known as the beer purity law. The original decree, declared in Bavaria in 1516, stated that beer could only be made with barley, hops and water. It was thought necessary to guard against adulteration of beer with inferior ingredients. Yeast was added to the list after its discovery.

**single-strain yeast** Yeast used for fermentation that consists of just one variety, as opposed to a mixture of strains.

**terroir** French for territory. A term borrowed from the wine industry to denote the properties of beer or hops that are specific to the geographical, climate and other physical characteristics of the area of production or growth.

**wild yeast** Yeast other than brewer's yeast present in the brewery environment. Produces beers with characteristics often reported as barnyard aromas, or as giving goaty or cheesy flavours.

**wort** The sugary liquid that results from the mashing process, in which, in the simplest case, the milled grains are soaked in water at about 67°C (153°F) for 90 minutes or so and then drained.

**Yorkshire square** A fermenting vessel invented in Yorkshire, in north-east England, and still in use in some traditional ale breweries. Originally consisting of a square base and a lower and upper deck, which helps separate the yeast from the beer. Said to produce dry, yet fruity beers.

# HOW BEER IS MADE

## the 30-second beer

**3-SECOND TASTER**
Beer is made from malted barley, water, hops and yeast, in a multi-stage process that can seem confusing, but has a beautifully simple logic to it.

**3-MINUTE BREW**
Each stage of the brewing process usually takes place in large, specialized vessels: water and malted barley are combined in the 'mash tun', and the resulting 'wort' is then run off into the 'kettle' or 'copper'. The hopped wort runs through a heat exchanger and then into fermentation vessels that are designed to keep yeast happy. But the basic process can be done on a stove top with a couple of large saucepans.

Any alcoholic drink is made by extracting fermentable sugar from fruit, grain or other substances such as honey, and giving yeast the right conditions to ferment that sugar into alcohol. For beer, the main grain used is barley, although any cereal can be used – wheat, maize and rice are also popular. Malted barley is steeped in hot water, which prompts enzymes in the grain to break down starch into fermentable sugars. These sugars, along with flavour compounds and other attributes, are rinsed out from the grain husks and dissolved into the water to create 'wort'. Hops are then added to the filtered wort and it's brought to the boil. This causes 'isomerization', a reaction in the hops' alpha acids that gives beer its bitterness as well as some anti-bacterial protection. More hops are added at the end of the boil so their essential oils aren't boiled off, and these add aroma and flavour that balance and complement the sugars and flavours of the malted barley. The hopped wort is then allowed to cool, before yeast is added. Over the next few days, yeast ferments most of the sugar to alcohol as well as adding its own flavour contribution. Other flavourings and adjuncts – such as herbs, fruit and spices – are sometimes used, but this is the basic template for beer.

**RELATED ENTRIES**
See also
FERMENTATION
page 50

HOPS
page 54

YEAST
page 60

WATER
page 62

**30-SECOND TEXT**
Pete Brown

*Beer can be made from just four ingredients: water, barley, hops and yeast, using appropriate vessels for each stage of the brewing process.*

# FERMENTATION

## the 30-second beer

**Humankind has harnessed** fermentation's beneficial properties for millennia, most notably in food production – bread, sauerkraut and cheese – and drinks making – beer, cider and wine. Sugars get gobbled up by the microbe responsible, be it yeast or bacteria, and this transforms both ingredients and flavours. Whether carboy or cask, Yorkshire square or conical fermenter, byproducts of yeast in brewing include carbon dioxide, heat and, of course, our friend alcohol. Yeasts are hungry little fungi, but they are picky about their environment: the liquid must be the right temperature, not too acidic and with just the right levels of salts and nutrients. While there are dozens of yeasts commercially available, historically brewers tend to opt for a few species: the warmth-loving *Saccharomyces cerevisiae*, which creates ales, and a couple of cooler kids, including *S. pastorianus* and *carlsbergensis*, responsible for lagers. There's also *Brettanomyces*, Brett for short, renowned for the edgy, often sour flavours it creates. Brewers can also leave it to nature, as the Belgians have done for centuries with their Lambic beers. Fermentation lasts anything from a week to several months. Once this phase has finished, there's the option of a secondary fermentation, often called conditioning, with or without additional yeasts and priming sugar.

**3-SECOND TASTER**
Fermentation converts sugar into alcohol, and with yeast in the driving seat it converts cooled wort into fresh beer, transforming flavours and creating a vast array of different beer styles.

**3-MINUTE BREW**
So what affects beer's flavour? Of course, the original wort. Then the yeast. Yeast breaks down simple sugars before tackling more complex ones. Along the way, it creates a range of flavour compounds, including esters, glycerol, phenols and so-called higher alcohols – there are over 40 of these in beer alone. Temperature is key: higher temperatures favour fruitier esters while cooler ones allow the hop fragrance to shine. Finally, adding dry hops during fermentation adds a whole new dimension.

**3-SECOND BIOGRAPHIES**
LOUIS PASTEUR
1822–95
As well as discovering how heat treatment could prevent spoilage, Pasteur convinced the scientific establishment that the cause of fermentation was yeast's action on sugars

DR JOHN EWALD SIEBEL
1845–1919
Brewing and educational pioneer who set up what became the Siebel Institute of Technology in 1872 in Chicago, designed 'to promote the progress of the industries based on fermentation'

**30-SECOND TEXT**
Susanna Forbes

*Higher temperatures during fermentation promote fruitier esters.*

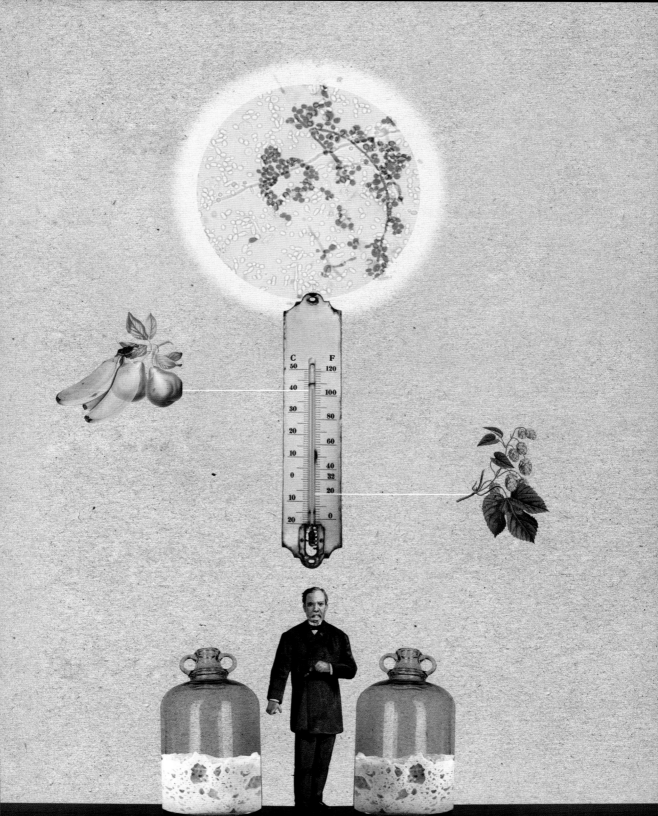

# CONDITIONING & MATURATION

## the 30-second beer

**RELATED ENTRIES**
See also
PACKAGING & DISPENSE
page 24

FERMENTATION
page 50

**30-SECOND TEXT**
Roger Protz

**Beer is too good to rush. It needs** care and attention to present it in the finest condition and this varies according to style. Ale is made faster than lager – but still needs time in the brewery before packaging. After fermentation, this 'green beer' needs to rest for several days in conditioning tanks while the beer purges itself of rough flavours that would leave yeasty and vegetable-like tastes. Beer may be treated differently after fermentation depending on how it will be packaged. Keg beer is often filtered and pasteurized to remove yeast and protein and is served using $CO_2$ pressure when it reaches pub or bar. But many modern craft keg brewers avoid these methods, which is why their beers are often served slightly cloudy. Pasteurization can leave a 'cardboard-like' flavour. Cask-conditioned beer (real ale) leaves the brewery unfinished. It undergoes secondary fermentation in the pub cellar, taking several days for the yeast to settle before it's ready to serve. Natural carbonation takes place to give the beer its sparkle, but real ale has to be served within two or three days or it will go flat. Bottled beer is usually filtered, but bottle-conditioned versions contain live yeast and may age over time, like wine. Many modern global lager brands are produced as quickly as ale but traditional lagers get several months conditioning at temperatures close to freezing.

**3-SECOND TASTER**
Beer needs time and care to reach perfection; even after fermentation it must be allowed to condition and mature – rushing it risks compromising quality and flavour.

**3-MINUTE BREW**
Conditioning and maturation relate to visual presentation but consumer attitudes are changing, and cloudy beer is becoming acceptable. Crystal-clear beers can be achieved by using 'finings' or isinglass, made from swim bladders of fish, which doesn't find favour with vegetarians and vegans. Many brewers have turned to alternatives, like Irish moss – a type of seaweed – or silica gel. The brewing faculty at Nottingham University in the UK is analysing hops to see if they can be used as a clearing agent.

*Beer needs to take its time, even after fermentation, before it is ready for you to drink.*

# HOPS

## the 30-second beer

**3-SECOND TASTER**
Hops play a three-fold role in brewing, most importantly adding bitterness but also preserving the beer, and infusing it with a rich tapestry of flavour and fragrance.

**3-MINUTE BREW**
Hops originated in China over a million years ago, with three species emerging. Two headed east while the other spread west to Europe. Central Europe was the first to realize hops' preservative potential in brewing. Hop gardens were first described in the eighth century in Hallertau, Germany, with the first recorded use in brewing being 822 CE, in Picardie, France. While Britain was slow to embrace hops, it soon became linked with several key beer styles, including bitter and IPA.

Spice, pine, herbs, citrus, peaches, flowers – just some of the flavours and aromas given to beer by hops. And it's all down to the rosebud-sized hop cone. Lupulin glands cling on the underside of tightly woven hop petals containing sticky, pollen-like grains packed with bittering alpha acids and fragrant essential oils. Part of the cannabis family, hops grow best between 35° and 55° latitude, preferring lengthy sunlight hours and well-drained soils. Every spring, the hop bines wind up the web of poles and wires, growing up to 10cm (4in) a day. Come autumn, skilled harvesters cut down the bines, separating off the cones before drying and packing them into hop bales weighing up to 65kg (143lb). Just like grapes and wine, hops have terroir. English bitter is synonymous with the earthy, spicy, grassy notes of Fuggles and Goldings; the herbal, floral fragrance of Saaz signifies Czech pilsner, while the bold citrus and pine flavours from Pacific Northwest hops suggest American pale ale. Globally, the acreage of hops planted is gently rising, with production figures fluctuating according to harvest conditions. The USA recently overtook Germany as the world's largest hop-growing region. While research used to focus on disease-resistant strains, now, thanks to the craft beer revolution, new aroma hops share the limelight.

**RELATED ENTRIES**
See also
ERNEST SALMON
page 56

AMERICAN CRAFT BEERS
page 86

**3-SECOND BIOGRAPHIES**
REGINALD SCOTT
1538–99
The first to write in depth on the English hop industry, his book *A Perfite Platform of a Hoppe Garden* (1576), covers every stage of cultivation

DR PETER DARBY
1956–
Developed numerous hops, including First Gold, Pilgrim and aphid-resistant Boadicea; revolutionized hop growing with breeding of hedge hop varieties

**30-SECOND TEXT**
Susanna Forbes

*For such tiny little 'flowers', hop cones can imbue beer with an incredible array of flavours, over and above their preservative and bittering properties.*

**1 June 1871**
Born Ernest Stanley Salmon at Richmond, Surrey

**1899**
Starts work as a researcher based at Kew Gardens, west London

**1903**
Reaches quarter-finals of men's singles at Wimbledon All England Tennis Club Championships

**1906**
Begins work at Wye College, then the University of London's School of Agriculture; plants batches of hop seedlings – the start of the hop development programme

**1917**
Receives cutting of 'wild Manitoban' hop from Canadian Professor W. T. Macoun, plants it and labels it BB1

**1918/19**
Harvests cones (flowers) and collects seeds from BB1, but the plant itself dies over the winter. Nevertheless he raises hundreds of its offspring in greenhouses

**1922**
Plants BB1 seedlings, including what would become Brewer's Gold, in the Wye College Nursery

**1934**
Brewer's Gold made available for commercial planting

**1937**
Salmon officially retires, but continues his hop breeding work

**1953**
Dr Ray Neve takes over Salmon's hop-breeding work at Wye College

**1955**
Salmon is awarded the Horace Brown brewing research medal by the UK's Institute of Brewing, for his hop-breeding work

**12 October 1959**
Salmon dies aged 89

**1981**
Dr Peter Darby joins Wye College, takes over from Ray Neve and continues the work Salmon started

**2007**
Hop breeding ceases at Wye College, but is saved and continues at China Farm, Kent thanks to Dr Darby and veteran hop grower Tony Redsell

**2016**
Salmon's last variety, OZ97a, finally gets a name (Ernest) and is highly feted as a British-grown, big flavour variety

# ERNEST SALMON

## The big-flavoured, modern

American hop varieties, used in so many pale ales regardless of where they're brewed, might not exist if it wasn't for Victorian Englishman, Ernest Salmon. Had he been a more dedicated tennis player the world might also have been denied the craft beer revolution, in which hop character has played no small part. Happily for beer lovers he hung up his racket and devoted himself to hop breeding.

Originally Salmon specialized in mycology and plant pathology – the study of fungi and plant diseases. He worked as a researcher at Kew Gardens, west London, focusing on powdery mildew, a fungal disease affecting many plants including hops. In 1906 he took a job as a hop breeder at Wye College, Kent and it was here he would make history in the world of hops and the beer industry.

Almost all the world's hop breeding and development efforts are based on Salmon's work. At one point about a third of global hop acreage came from his cultivars and, arguably, many of the most popular hop varieties would not exist were it not for him.

Each hop seed can grow into an entirely new variety of hop, so plants are bred from cuttings and crossed by applying pollen from one variety to another, which can create a lineage much like a human family tree. Growing hops from seed can also be a part of a breeding programme, but once the grower creates or discovers a viable variety it will be propagated from cuttings.

Salmon was sent a cutting of a wild hop from Canada (known as a wild 'Manitoban'). He planted it and labelled it BB1. It produced flowers from which he collected seeds, but soon died. Its seedlings were much more successful. One would become a variety he named Brewer's Gold and, a few seasons on, led to a hop called Northern Brewer. These are said to be the source of all the world's bitter hop varieties.

Key to hop bitterness and 'keeping quality' is what is known as 'alpha acid' – part of the resin that is found in a hop's lupulin gland. Higher alpha acids are characteristic of the flavoursome American hops that have fuelled the craft beer movement. When Salmon began his work, hops averaged at most 6% alpha acid. Today there are hop breeders releasing varieties with more than 20%. It's said that all of these derive from Brewer's Gold.

*Sophie Atherton*

# MALT

## the 30-second beer

Alcohol is made when yeast eats sugar. Broadly speaking, ferment fruit and you get wine; ferment grain and you get beer. But before you can brew, you need to malt the grain, basically tricking it into activating enzymes that will convert its starch into fermentable sugar. At the end of malting, the grain is dried in a kiln. Lightly kiln it and you get pale malt. Apply more heat and you get darker malts, but go too dark and you kill the enzymes and the grain won't ferment. But you do get lots of luscious flavour: crystal malt is chewy and granola-like, and dark malts have hints of berry fruit, coffee, chocolate or tobacco. Most beers consist of 90% pale malt to provide the sugar that ferments to alcohol, and the remaining mix determines whether you get pale and crisp or darker, chewier beers. You can make beer with other grains such as wheat, oats or spelt, but barley is king. And while the malting process gives beer its style and character, the strain of barley that goes into malting makes a big difference, too. Barley varieties are carefully bred for their character and yield. Maris Otter, first bred in 1964, is considered to be peerless by many ale brewers for its superb flavour.

**RELATED ENTRIES**
See also
BEER & THE INDUSTRIAL REVOLUTION
page 36

ORIGINS OF MODERN ALES
page 40

HOW BEER IS MADE
page 48

**3-SECOND BIOGRAPHY**
EDWARD SLOPER BEAVEN
1857–1941
Pioneer of modern barley breeding, Beaven's work at Warminster maltings in the late nineteenth and early twentieth century led to the first commercial barley varieties and essentially gave birth to modern malt

**30-SECOND TEXT**
Pete Brown

**3-SECOND TASTER**
Beer's core ingredient is malted barley – the malting process is vital for getting fermentable sugar, but it also creates a rainbow of different flavours.

**3-MINUTE BREW**
Technically, beer is the result of fermenting any grain. Every civilization in history was founded on achieving a supply of one of the noble grains known as cereals. Coincidence? I don't think so. Humans figured out how to malt barley for brewing roughly 10,000 years ago, by pure trial and error, with no knowledge of enzymes or how the process activated them. That's determination for you.

*The sugars that are needed to make the alcohol in beer are often provided by malted barley, although other cereals are sometimes used.*

# YEAST

## the 30-second beer

Yeast is a single-celled organism that is neither plant nor animal, but part of the fungus kingdom. Yeasts are some of the earliest living organisms on earth. About 1,500 different species have currently been identified, and these are estimated to account for just 1% of all fungus species. From beer's point of view, the most important species is *Saccharomyces* (a literal translation of the words 'sugar fungus' into Latin), which is known for converting sugar into alcohol and carbon dioxide. There are several *species* of *Saccharomyces*, which each in turn contain many *strains*. *Saccharomyces cerevisiae* (usually written more handily as *S. cerevisiae*) is the dominant species used for brewing beer as well as for fermenting grapes into wine and baking bread. As well as making this apparently simple conversion, yeast can also contribute flavour compounds, some of which are seen as desirable, others less so. In the wild, a yeast sample will contain many different strains or species within it. The work of Louis Pasteur and Emil Christian Hansen led to the cultivation of single-strain yeasts in laboratories that ensure consistent, controllable flavour. But there's now increasing interest among craft brewers in so-called 'wild yeasts' such as *Brettanomyces* ('British fungus'), which can contribute dry, earthy, sharp or sour flavours to beer.

### 3-SECOND TASTER
Yeast is the most important element in brewing, the agent that converts all the other ingredients into beer.

### 3-MINUTE BREW
Given its microscopic nature, the discovery of yeast – and its role in fermentation – took centuries. Early brewers used to think of fermentation as a magical process, and the foamy deposit that grew on top of fermenting ale was referred to in Britain as 'godisgoode'. Even after yeast was first identified and described, it took over 200 years to conclusively prove that these microscopic blobs were responsible for fermentation.

### RELATED ENTRIES
See also
ALE VERSUS LAGER
page 18

HOW BEER IS MADE
page 48

FERMENTATION
page 50

### 3-SECOND BIOGRAPHY
ANTONIE VAN LEEUWENHOEK
1632–1723
Dutch draper who revolutionized lens technology and became known as the 'Father of Microbiology'. He was the first to identify and draw yeast cells in beer, but didn't know what they were, or what they contributed

### 30-SECOND TEXT
Pete Brown

*It took humans a very long time to understand yeast and what it does; Antonie van Leeuwenhoek (pictured) was the first to draw yeast cells in beer, but he had no idea what they were.*

# WATER

## the 30-second beer

When you raise a glass of beer to your lips, are you aware that around 90% of the liquid is water? Water is often overlooked by drinkers but not by brewers, who treat it with due reverence. They don't call it water – that's used for washing vessels and floors. The liquid that plays a crucial role in the brewing process is called liquor. Water is the result of rain falling on the earth and percolating through soil and rock until it settles on a water table. During that journey, the water absorbs mineral salts, and the level and type of salts have an important impact on the beer being brewed. Modern lagers are based on the first golden version of the style brewed in Pilsen in Bohemia in the nineteenth century – hence pilsner. These have a satiny smoothness and are made with water with a low level of salts: the level of salts in the water in Pilsen is 30.8 parts per million. In sharp contrast, the waters of the Trent Valley in England are rich in salts: 1,226 parts per million. The area is home to Burton-on-Trent, world-famous as the town where pale ale and IPA were created in the nineteenth century. Today brewers worldwide who brew pale ale 'Burtonize' their liquor, adding gypsum and magnesium salts to replicate the true pale-ale style.

**RELATED ENTRIES**
See also
ALE VERSUS LAGER
page 18

PALE ALES
page 70

**30-SECOND TEXT**
Roger Protz

**3-SECOND TASTER**
Water is critical for brewing and varies according to geography – soft water is ideal for lager; hard water, rich in mineral salts, is ideal for pale ale.

**3-MINUTE BREW**
One of the great brewing myths is that Guinness in Dublin uses water from the River Liffey to make its famous stouts. The Liffey is tidal and would need to be heavily filtered and cleaned to remove waste. In fact, the brewery uses pure water drawn from the Wicklow Mountains. Brewers who use public water clean and filter it to remove impurities and unwanted chemicals.

*Differences in water used for brewing can affect the flavour and mouthfeel of the finished beer much more than many drinkers realize.*

# SPECIALITY BREWING

## the 30-second beer

**3-SECOND TASTER**
Brewers are updating old brewing methods and ingredients in a quest to innovate, proving there's nothing new under the tun.

**3-MINUTE BREW**
Farmhouse beers were once widespread across northern Europe and are re-emerging, but rarely commercially. Norwegian 'raw' beers are brewed using unboiled wort and fermented by 'kveik' yeasts. Finnish sahti uses few or no hops but strains the wort through juniper twigs. Swedish Gotlandsdricka is similar. The limits of beer are being pushed by Sweden's Omnipollo and others. Creative use of grains and natural flavour essences and ingredients such as marshmallows and lactose make dessert-like beers.

**After brewers discovered hops** and got the hang of consistent fermentation, beers not made with time-honoured ingredients and methods started to die out. In recent years, interest in such beers has rekindled, as modern brewers look to expand their repertoires. Something has to balance beer's natural sweetness. Before hops took over, herbs and spices were used. Now, sweet gale, heather, spruce tips and herb blends (gruit) add exciting flavours. Coriander seeds are widely used in Belgian wheat beers and Gose, while cinnamon, chilli and coffee regularly find a home in stouts and porters. Demand for sour beers is increasing. Here, fermentation is by various mixes of yeasts: brewer's yeast, wild yeasts and bacteria strains, such as *Lactobacillus* and *Pediococcus*, which produce a lactic acid tartness, while wild yeasts add an attractive mustiness. For Belgium's classic sour Lambic beers, the souring micro-organisms are allowed in from the atmosphere for 'spontaneous fermentation'. Other brewers add them by hand. All kinds of fruit and honey are added to beers so yeasts can feast and leave behind added flavour in Lambics, American IPAs and pale ales, and British ales. You name it, it's been added to beer. Even old-fashioned milk stout, sweetened with unfermentable lactose, has been re-invented as pastry beer, with added flavours for dessert-like effects.

**RELATED ENTRIES**
See also
CONDITIONING & MATURATION
page 52

SOUR BEERS
page 84

OTHER SIGNIFICANT STYLES
page 88

**3-SECOND BIOGRAPHIES**
JEAN-PIERRE VAN ROY
1942–
Third-generation brewer at Belgian Lambic brewery, Cantillon

HENOK FENTIE
1980–
Swedish former homebrewer and joint founder of Omnipollo, a 'phantom' brewery that uses breweries in Belgium, the UK and the USA, often to make beers that are the antithesis of the Reinheitsgebot beer 'purity' law

**30-SECOND TEXT**
Jerry Bartlett

*Brewers love to stretch the notion of what a beer can be to bring us new flavours and styles.*

# BEER STYLES

## BEER STYLES
### GLOSSARY

**ABV** Alcohol By Volume. Usually expressed as % ABV. The percentage of alcohol by volume in a beer.

**barley wine** An ale of British origin, usually amber to bronze in colour. Named because of its wine-like strength, around 8–12% ABV, and predominant malted barley flavour. (Usually less bitter than equivalent strength IPAs.)

**bière de garde** Originally, brewed in farmhouse breweries in northern France in the cooler months to sustain farm workers in the summer months when, in the days before refrigeration, no brewing took place. Usually malty and relatively strong.

**Bock** A malty, sweetish lager of around 6–7% ABV, blond to chestnut in colour, originally from Einbeck, Germany. There are stronger versions (Doppelbock and Eisbock) as well as seasonal variations including Maibock (for May). Weizenbock is a warm-fermented variant.

**craft beer** A term that originated in the USA and which meant beer produced by the small, independent breweries founded since the late 1970s – as opposed to mass-produced lagers. Now used far beyond the USA. Usually (but not exclusively) denotes beer in the style of, or inspired by, American craft brewers. Confusingly, it is also increasingly employed as a marketing term by larger established breweries for sub-brands (some of which are made using separate, smaller brewing facilities) to give the impression of being an independent brewery. The definition of craft beer is contentious, especially in the UK, but many beer enthusiasts see it as being about the ethos and intent of the brewer, especially one dedicated to making beer that puts quality before market share.

**double** Also called 'dubbel' (from the Flemish), a Belgian beer style the invention of which is attributed to Trappist brewery Westmalle but is now widespread. The name derives from its supposed relative strength to standard beers. Most examples are around 6–8% ABV, dark red-brown in colour with rich malt, restrained hops and yeast-influenced character.

**Dunkel** German for dark. Denoting a brown, to dark brown beer, as compared to a Helles, which is pale to golden.

**Gose** A wheat beer flavoured with coriander and brewed using salt or salty water. Originating from the Leipzig area of Germany, its popularity has increased in recent years.

**gruit**  A blend of hedgerow herbs used to flavour and season ales before the use of hops became widespread.

**IPA**  Stands for India Pale Ale; a stronger version of the pale ale style.

**Lambic**  Acidic-tasting (sour) wheat beers from the Brussels area of Belgium fermented by wild yeasts and bacteria allowed to settle on the wort cooling in open vessels in a process known as spontaneous fermentation. A blend of Lambics of different ages is called 'Gueuze'.

**Märzen**  A stronger lager, traditionally brewed in March (*März* in German) before the once-decreed brewing close season that lasted from 23 April to 29 September and often associated with Munich's Oktoberfest.

**saison**  An ale style (belonging to the farmhouse ales family) originating from Belgium, where it was historically brewed as a seasonal beer to refresh the farm workers. Saisons are characterized as refreshing, dry, and highly carbonated.

**Schwarzbier**  German for 'black beer'. A dark lager, ranging in colour from very dark brown to almost black because it contains dark roasted malts that give it a toasted, slightly burnt flavour.

**session IPA**  An ale that has the hoppy bitterness of a modern American-style IPA, but which is not as strong in alcohol, making it more suitable for drinking several in one sitting – a session.

**Trappist**  Denoting beers brewed at a Trappist monastery recognized by the International Trappist Association. Trappist beers are often strong (7–10% ABV) and conform to styles originating in Belgium. Beers brewed in similar styles but not at one of these monasteries are known as Abbey-style beers.

**triple**  Another Trappist invention, stronger than a double, but at around 8–10% ABV, not triple the standard strength. Golden in colour, drier and hoppier than a double. Also known as tripel, from the Flemish.

**wild yeast**  Yeast varieties that live in the natural environment and have not been cultivated for use in breweries or bakeries. Some breweries use them to ferment their beers because they impart unusual but often desirable flavours.

# PALE ALES

## the 30-second beer

Pale ale revolutionized brewing not only in Britain but throughout the world in the nineteenth century. The style was made possible by the new technologies of the Industrial Revolution, when commercial coke production on a large scale led to it replacing wood as the fuel used in maltings. The result was pale rather than brown malt. India Pale Ale (IPA) was developed in London and Burton-on-Trent to meet a demand from the British in India for a more refreshing beer than dark milds, porters and stouts. IPAs were strong in alcohol and a lower gravity version – pale ale – was developed for the domestic market. Both IPA and pale ale were brewed using just pale malt and brewing sugar, and were heavily hopped. They were also aged before they were ready for consumption but when brewers started to build large pub estates they wanted beer that could be brewed and served quickly. The result was 'running beer' that had just a short conditioning in the pub cellar. It was dubbed 'bitter' by drinkers and it remains the most popular British beer style. While pale ale and bitter are low in strength they are well hopped, giving the beers fine floral, peppery or spicy aromas and flavours, balanced by juicy and honeyed malts.

**RELATED ENTRIES**
See also
BEER & THE INDUSTRIAL REVOLUTION
page 36

MALT
page 58

WATER
page 62

**30-SECOND TEXT**
Roger Protz

**3-SECOND TASTER**
Pale ale and its big brother India Pale Ale changed the face of brewing in the nineteenth century and it even influenced lager brewing in central Europe.

**3-MINUTE BREW**
In the late twentieth century a number of British brewers developed golden ale, a new style of pale beer. Unlike modern bitters and pale ales, which often blend darker crystal malt with pale malt, golden ales are as pale as lager. Many brewers use American, European and Australasian hops in golden ale and as a result it has a fruity/citrus character quite different to pale ale.

*Pale ales were groundbreaking when first invented and are still making waves in the world of beer today.*

# STOUT & PORTER

## the 30-second beer

In eighteenth-century London, drinkers developed a taste for beers with a smoky character, made using malt dried over open flames. This beer was often aged to allow smoke to diffuse but ageing also turned the beer sour. For balance, a mix of aged sour beer and fresh smoky beer went on sale and became popular, it seems, with the porters of London who lent their name to the drink. Stronger versions of 'porter' were called stout porter – stout for short. The development of smoke-free pale malt – which also provided more brewing sugar than smoky malts – saw pennywise brewers switch ingredients, using mostly pale malt and maintaining the dark colour and roasted notes with a small amount of dark malt or roasted, unmalted barley. Hence, the nature of both stout and porter changed over time, especially as the ageing process became less significant. Today, stouts and porters – the names are now largely interchangeable – come in a variety of styles. Irish stout has a dry, bitter note from roasted barley, while milk stout includes lactose for creaminess and extra body. Oatmeal stouts feature oats for a silky character and imperial Russian stouts are both strong and well hopped – a legacy of the days when these beers were exported across the Baltic, and alcohol and hops helped keep the beer fresh.

### RELATED ENTRIES
See also
ORIGINS OF MODERN ALES
page 40

MALT
page 58

ARTHUR GUINNESS
page 78

### 3-SECOND BIOGRAPHY
CATHERINE THE GREAT
1729–96
Beer-loving Empress of Russia whose courtiers in St Petersburg were big consumers of exported strong British stout, which thus became known as 'imperial Russian stout'

### 30-SECOND TEXT
Jeff Evans

### 3-SECOND TASTER
Stout and porter are related beers that have changed character considerably since their early popularity in eighteenth-century London.

### 3-MINUTE BREW
A story is told about a wily brewer named Ralph Harwood who, it is said, invented porter. Noting that drinkers often enjoyed a mix of beers and, seeing publicans racing from cask to cask to meet their request, Harwood reportedly invented a beer served from one cask that achieved the same effect. However, while the idea of blending beers seems accurate, there is evidence that the term 'porter' existed some time before Harwood's possible intervention.

*Guinness may be the most famous example of the style, but it wasn't the first – and it isn't the last word on stout or porter.*

# STRONG BEERS

## the 30-second beer

### Want to show off? Choose and

share a high ABV beer with a friend! Barley wines, and old and vintage ales give the brewer the canvas with which to display a wonderful depth and variety of flavours. To raise the alcohol levels in a beer, as well as additional malts, brewers need to help the yeast. Either they add in more yeast, or they find one that can cope with a higher alcohol environment, or, as with Eisbock, they 'jack' the beer, partially freezing it, removing some water and concentrating it. While care is needed to avoid contamination, wild yeasts can often ferment further than their conventional cousins, adding in unusual flavours, too. Colours in old, strong beers can range from deep gold through to midnight black and the flavour spectrum is almost limitless. Think rich Christmas cake-filled aromas with sultanas and plums, vanilla and spices in an aged barley wine, or vinous, tangy, almost sour notes in a beer that's been barrel matured. Sometimes there's a savoury, umami flavour from time spent on the lees, and if there are dark malts, expect coffee, nuts and dark chocolate, too. Originally a 'must' for all fashionable aristocracy in Great Britain, barley wines in Britain tend to be mostly about the malt whereas hops are more prominent in America. With a carefully selected recipe each year, beers like the highly prized Fuller's Vintage Ale repay careful cellaring.

**3-SECOND TASTER**
With their fabulous richness, strong beers offer a chance to celebrate the brewer's skill and, like wine, the chance to cellar and age them for drinking at a later date.

**3-MINUTE BREW**
Cornish Brewery Company kicked off the world's strongest beer wars in 1986 using three different yeasts to reach 16%. Sam Adams' Utopias arrived in 2002. Now 28%, its multi-yeast strategy includes a 'Ninja' yeast, able to withstand high ABV conditions, plus a range of barrels for ageing. In the late 2000s, German brewer Schorschbräu took on BrewDog as both began 'jacking' (fractional freezing) their beers. In 2011, Schorschbock 57 (57%) won, just ahead of BrewDog's End of History (55%).

**RELATED ENTRIES**
See also
ALCOHOLIC STRENGTH
page 20

CONDITIONING & MATURATION
page 52

STOUT & PORTER
page 72

BELGIAN STYLES
page 80

**3-SECOND BIOGRAPHIES**
JOHN KEELING
1956–
Former head brewer at Fuller's. Established Fuller's Vintage Ale as one of the world's finest, most age-worthy beers

MENNO OLIVIER
1963–
Founder of de Molen in the Netherlands, the brewery behind Bommen & Granatan, an extraordinary barley wine

**30-SECOND TEXT**
Susanna Forbes

*Strong ales offer some of the richest, most intense flavour experiences.*

# LAGERS
## the 30-second beer

### Over 90% of the world's beer

consists of variations on one style: pale, golden 'pilsner' lager. Pilsner Urquell (literal translation, the 'original pilsner') was created by Josef Groll in the Czech town of Plzen in 1842, and the style spread rapidly, spawning so many imitators, that 'pilsner' or 'Pilsener' became the world's dominant beer style by the end of the nineteenth century. Most big commercial brands in countries across the globe are blander interpretations of the style than the original, noted for being cold, crisp and refreshing, with a very light, delicate flavour. This is what most people regard as beer, certainly as lager. But in its heartland of central Europe, there's much more to lager than this commercialized juggernaut. A true pilsner from the Czech Republic or Germany still has a clean, subtle character, but has a satisfying dryness and a distinct grassy or citrus hop character. Munich-style Helles looks similar to pilsner but is slightly sweet, with lower bitterness. And lager existed long before pilsner. Vienna-style lagers are amber, with slightly more caramel character. Märzen and Bock are stronger and seasonal, while German Dunkel and Schwarzbier can be dark brown or almost black, have a fuller flavour, but still retain some of lager's crisp lightness.

**RELATED ENTRIES**
See also
ALE VERSUS LAGER
page 18

JOSEF GROLL
page 38

CONDITIONING &
MATURATION
page 52

GERMANY
page 98

**3-SECOND BIOGRAPHY**
GABRIEL SEDLMAYR
1772–1839
Brewer at the Spaten Brewery in Munich, who copied British pale-ale brewing techniques and applied them to lager for the first time, creating the basis for what Josef Groll then developed into pilsner lager

**30-SECOND TEXT**
Pete Brown

*Lager is one of brewing's nomadic migrants, starting life in Europe, travelling across the Atlantic and spreading throughout the world.*

**3-SECOND TASTER**
Lager is much-maligned and abused, but beyond the obvious brands there's a wonderful variety of style and character to discover.

**3-MINUTE BREW**
Because good-quality lager should ideally be stored at low temperatures for several weeks, it's more expensive to brew than ale and requires more equipment. This, plus mainstream lager's poor reputation among discerning drinkers, means that the range of lager styles hasn't yet been fully explored by craft brewers and drinkers. But lager's delicacy leaves nowhere for faults to hide, making lager an intriguing and increasingly attractive challenge for ambitious craft brewers.

**28 September 1725**
Arthur Guinness born at Celbridge, County Kildare

**1752**
Inherits £100 from his godfather Archbishop Price, which he uses to start brewing ale in Leixlip, County Kildare, around 16km (10 miles) from Dublin

**1759**
Moves to Dublin, signing a 9,000-year lease on a disused brewery at St James's Gate for a rent of £45 per year

**1769**
Starts exporting his beer by sending six-and-a-half barrels to England; begins brewing porter soon after

**1799**
Ceases brewing any beer but porter

**23 January 1803**
Arthur Guinness dies; brewery business taken over by his son Arthur Guinness II (1768–1855)

**1821**
Recipe for Extra Superior Porter, today known as Guinness Original or Extra Stout and usually only available in bottles, is officially written down, having already been brewed for a number of years

**1959**
Draught Guinness – the version of the beer found in most bars in the UK, Ireland and beyond – is created. It's the world's first 'nitro beer', dispensed using a mixture of nitrogen gas and carbon dioxide. Its distinctive 'surge and settle' effect is down to scientist Michael Ash

**1997**
Guinness Plc merges with Grand Metropolitan Plc in a £24 billion deal. The new company is called Diageo Plc

**2014–15**
The Guinness story comes full circle, when the brewery once again starts making beers other than porter/stout. The Brewer's Project pilot brewery adds a golden ale and a lager to the range

# ARTHUR GUINNESS

Mention stout and most people still think of Guinness. It's considered quintessentially Irish, the drink always raised to celebrate St Patrick's Day and quaffed by Dubliners since time immemorial. But the Guinness most people are familiar with is a more recent phenomenon than they might imagine – and not as Irish as it could be.

Guinness owes its origins to eighteenth-century London. Dark beers were popular, widespread and enjoyed by porters who unloaded ships and carried goods around town for delivery. Hence the beer became known as porter. 'Stout porters' were stronger porters and eventually this was abbreviated to stout.

The man, or rather one of the men, behind the drink which to many is synonymous with 'stout' was Arthur Guinness. His story begins in 1750s Ireland; Arthur learned to brew in his stepmother's pub. He wasn't rich and only managed to start his own small, rural brewery thanks to money left to him by his godfather. He ran it for more than five years before moving to Dublin, where some relatives already had successful businesses.

The new location would turn out to be of major importance, not least because it offered the opportunity to more easily export beer.

Arthur Guinness put his now famous signature (since trademarked and used widely on Guinness's visual branding) on a 9,000-year lease for his new brewery on New Year's Eve 1759. The site was actually fairly dilapidated with little in the way of brewing kit, so it's not surprising that it took another 10 years to build up trade and begin exporting to England. Soon after this he had his first crack at brewing porter. Slow but steady progress meant that 30 years later, in 1799, he stopped brewing other types of beer and focused solely on porter. Different versions were brewed for different markets. This included West India Porter, still brewed and popular in Asia, Africa and the Caribbean, but now known as Foreign Extra Stout.

Arthur Guinness died in 1803 leaving a successful business for his son, also named Arthur, to build upon. By the 1830s his St James's Gate Brewery was the largest in Ireland, exporting beer across three continents. But the famous draught Guinness – the one largely responsible for the hijacking of the style that is stout – wasn't invented until 1959. It was created to commemorate Arthur's move to Dublin and has turned out to be a rather fitting memorial.

*Sophie Atherton*

# BELGIAN STYLES

## the 30-second beer

That a small country like Belgium is considered a great brewing nation is down to the diversity of beer styles it has managed to preserve. Britain and Germany may have hundreds of beers, but they are variations on a few themes. Belgium has perhaps 12 distinct families, most of which could be subdivided. Belgian beers sometimes use sugar, fruit or spices, but everything, even hops, takes a back seat to fermentation. Belgian styles capitalize on yeasts that produce a complex range of flavours, and warm fermentation in various, often intricate procedures: multi-stage warm fermentation, long barrel ageing, cool conditioning, bottle conditioning, as well as spontaneous fermentation. Belgium's Trappist monasteries and abbeys produce strong, flavourful brews fermented multiple times to produce dark, rich 'doubles' and pale, dry 'triples'. Wallonia's saisons are originally farmhouse-brewed seasonals, as were Bière de Garde in French Flanders. Saison yeast produces highly carbonated, crisp and refreshing beers compared to their maltier French cousins. There are strong golden ales, some of ordinary strength. Strong, malty scotch ales are often produced for Christmas. All styles are dominated in quantity by golden lagers, which might have eradicated all in their path if it hadn't been for the persistence of a couple of foreign beer writers championing their cause.

**RELATED ENTRIES**
See also
WHEAT BEERS
page 82

SOUR BEERS
page 84

BELGIUM
page 96

MICHAEL JACKSON
page 102

**3-SECOND TASTER**
Belgium's diverse range of styles includes many strong and flavourful beers that gain their distinctiveness from special yeasts and often complex fermentation.

**3-MINUTE BREW**
After touring Belgium in the 1970s, British beer writer Michael Jackson and later, Tim Webb, eulogized Belgian beer beyond its borders. Exports increased, especially to the USA, establishing as world class the Trappist breweries Orval, Chimay and Westmalle, and the classic saison producer Dupont. Undoubtedly, this helped small Belgian breweries survive and prosper. Then, as part of the craft beer movement, American breweries such as New Belgium emerged to produce their own interpretations of Belgian styles.

**3-SECOND BIOGRAPHIES**
PETER CROMBECQ
1956–
Belgian beer and genealogy writer and founder of consumer organization De Objectieve Bierproevers (The Objective Beer Tasters), and champion of beers of the Benelux region

TIM WEBB
1956–
British writer known for his expertise on the beers of Belgium

**30-SECOND TEXT**
Jerry Bartlett

*Belgium's wide range of traditional beer styles has influenced many a modern brewer.*

# WHEAT BEERS

## the 30-second beer

Wheat beer is an ancient and venerable member of the ale family that dates back to antiquity. Some 6,000 years ago wheat beers were brewed in Egypt, Mesopotamia and Sumeria. Wheat beer is most closely associated today with Bavaria in southern Germany, where it's the most popular style with drinkers. In the sixteenth century, wheat beer production became a royal monopoly: the masses were allowed to drink barley-based beer while the nobility consumed paler and more refined wheat beer known as 'weiss', meaning white. The monopoly was gradually relaxed, and commercial wheat beers were brewed from the eighteenth and nineteenth centuries. The style went into steep decline with the rise of lager beer but enjoyed a remarkable recovery in the late nineteenth century when it was taken up by young drinkers who saw it as a healthier style than lager. As a result of the yeast used, Bavarian wheat beer has a pronounced aroma and flavour of cloves and Juicy Fruit bubblegum. The beers are lightly hopped. Wheat beer is also popular in Belgium, where sales took off as a result of the popularity of one brand, Hoegaarden. The beer is a blend of malted barley, unmalted wheat, hops, coriander and curaçao orange peel. Other Belgian brewers add fruit and spice to their interpretations of the style.

### RELATED ENTRY
See also
GERMANY
page 98

### 3-SECOND BIOGRAPHY
PIERRE CELIS
1925–2011
Revived wheat beer in Belgium. He had worked at the last wheat beer brewery in Hoegaarden and when it closed, he bought some brewing equipment and recreated the beer with enormous success. When a fire destroyed the brewery, Celis accepted financial support from Stella Artois to rebuild the plant

### 30-SECOND TEXT
Roger Protz

### 3-SECOND TASTER
Wheat beer is an ancient style that dates back to the time of the pharaohs. The main producers of wheat beer today are found in Bavaria and Belgium.

### 3-MINUTE BREW
Wheat beer is something of a misnomer, as it's brewed with a blend of malted barley and wheat. Wheat doesn't have a husk and can cause problems when used in brewing: barley, with its tough husk, prevents wheat from clogging pipes. In Bavaria, drinkers prefer the naturally cloudy, unfiltered version of wheat beer known as 'hefeweisse' – with yeast – though there are filtered versions called Kristall.

*Wheat beer has a long history, including falling out of fashion, then a revival into an iconic style.*

# SOUR BEERS

## the 30-second beer

Your first taste of an intentionally sour beer can be a shock, if all you've ever tried is conventional beers. But really, a sour beer is just more acidic, like dry white wine or cider. Over the centuries, where most other brewing countries got rid of the sourness in their beers, Belgium turned sour beers into an art form. Its Lambic beers from the Brussels area are spontaneously fermented by the airborne wild yeasts and bacteria allowed to drift into the brewery and set to work on the cooling, unfermented beer left open to the winds. The sourness in the red ales of West Flanders and the brown ales of East Flanders comes from the mixed yeast and microbial culture added physically/deliberately to the unfermented beer. The art in sour beer making comes in maturing the beer, usually in oak barrels. Young Lambics are too sharp and older ones too flat, so different ages are blended and bottled to become Gueuze, getting a Champagne-like spritz from fermentation in the bottle. If cherries are added to a Lambic it becomes Kriek; raspberries make Framboise. Two old German styles are becoming popular again, both mildly tart, light, easy-drinking wheat beers: Berliner Weisse, often flavoured with fruit or spices, and Gose, distinctive because of the addition of coriander and salt.

*Refreshing tartness is the goal in sour beers, often balanced by fruit and other flavours.*

# AMERICAN CRAFT BEERS

## the 30-second beer

### 3-SECOND TASTER
American brewers created
their own take on pale
ale and IPA to showcase
American-grown hops and
kick-started a worldwide
craft beer movement.

### 3-MINUTE BREW
Because of the near
ubiquity of IPAs in the
USA, sub-genres and
regional variations create
diversity. East Coast IPAs
are rounder and not as
mouth-puckering as West
Coast ones, while soft,
hazy, New England IPAs
pack their huge fruitiness
from massive amounts of
dry hopping. Then there
are double (or imperial)
and even triple IPAs,
which ramp up alcohol
levels, while session
IPAs dial them down.

If a love of traditional European beer styles ignited the American craft beer movement in the late 1970s, it was the creation of American IPA that turned it into a revolution. The seeds of this revolution came from new American hop varieties like Cascade, with its intense flavours of grapefruit and pine resin. When Sierra Nevada used Cascade in its pale ale, a new style was born. In turn, the American version of IPA was stronger, bolder, more bitter and more aromatic than contemporary British versions. Emerging around 1985, by the turn of the millennium, American IPAs dominated the craft scene as the perfect style to show off the flavours and aromas offered by an ever-increasing range of hops: Chinook, Citra, Amarillo, Simcoe, and so on. Brewers never lost sight of other styles. The Great American Beer Festival's competition runs to almost 100 categories – 20 containing 'American-style' in the name. Beer rating sites show a fascination for big styles like imperial stouts and porters and using barrel ageing to impart flavours to the beer from the barrels' previous contents (whiskies, wines, and so on). Breweries sprang up to create American interpretations of Belgian sour styles, and used exotic yeasts like *Brettanomyces*. American craft beers reflect both a desire for beer style authenticity and a compulsion to push frontiers.

### RELATED ENTRIES
See also
UNITED STATES
page 104

CRAFT BEER
page 120

GARRETT OLIVER
page 144

### 3-SECOND BIOGRAPHIES
KEN GROSSMAN
1954–
Founded the Sierra Nevada
Brewing Company in Chico,
California, now one of the top
10 craft breweries in the USA

SAM CALAGIONE
1970–
Founded Dogfish Head in 1995
in Delaware. Known for creating
'extreme' beers: unusually
strong or which use unusual
ingredients. His ideas have
become widespread in
craft beer

### 30-SECOND TEXT
Jerry Bartlett

*The hop-fuelled craft beer revolution in the USA has made it arguably the world's leading beer nation.*

# OTHER SIGNIFICANT STYLES

## the 30-second beer

### The USA-based Beer Judge

Certification Program (BJCP) identifies well over 100 different styles of beer – and acknowledges it doesn't cover every style! Nevertheless, its widely used guidelines help illustrate how many types of beer there are. Within each style are hundreds of individual interpretations of the given type of beer. The most notable and prevalent styles are covered in the preceding pages. Get to know these and you can go on an incredible voyage of discovery within them. Beyond that there's a world of speciality, seasonal and other beers to explore. Those described as 'speciality' usually involve ingredients that add flavour in addition to hops. Chilli beers might sound whacky but can be a marvellous match for food. Coffee beers, often brewed in collaboration with independent roasteries, are a widespread phenomenon. Genuinely seasonal beers are only made at the time of year that the relevant ingredient is harvested. Pumpkin and green hop beers are two good examples. The autumnal squash forms part of the mash of pumpkin beers, with spices added later. Hops are usually dried at harvest time for use throughout the year ahead. Green hops (also referred to as 'wet' or 'fresh') must go into the brew just hours after being picked and create a characteristic light freshness in the beer.

**RELATED ENTRY**
See also
SPECIALITY BREWING
page 64

**3-SECOND TASTER**
There are more than 100 different styles of beer and hundreds of versions of each style are brewed around the world.

**3-MINUTE BREW**
Even though the barley used in beer is naturally low in gluten, many brewers use enzymes to make gluten-free versions, safe for coeliacs. There are also beers made from alternative, gluten-free grains such as sorghum, buckwheat and millet. Not a fan of hops? Although very niche, there are brewers who still make beers flavoured with a mixture of herbs and spices known as 'gruit', which usually includes bog myrtle and yarrow among its ingredients.

**3-SECOND BIOGRAPHIES**
DEREK GREEN
1940–
The man behind Green's, one of the early pioneers of commercially available gluten-free beer. In 2004, after teaming up with a Belgian professor, he released a beer made with alternative grains. The range also includes brews made with de-glutenized barley

BRUCE WILLIAMS
1960–
Founded Williams Bros Brewery, which makes famous heather ale, Fraoch, essentially a gruit (although it includes some hops). He got the 4,000-year-old recipe from a woman who came to his Glasgow homebrew shop in the late 1980s; she agreed to share the recipe in return for learning how to brew it

**30-SECOND TEXT**
Sophie Atherton

*Much of beer's versatility as a drink stems from the wide variety of styles.*

# BEER CULTURE

**brewpub**  A pub or bar containing brewing equipment of sufficient capacity to make beer for sale on the premises.

**cask ale**  Ale that has been matured and conditioned in a cask without having been pasteurized and with little or no filtration. As live yeast remains, the beer continues to ferment slowly, providing a light, natural carbonation when the beer is served. It is not dispensed using carbon dioxide ($CO_2$), as is the case with other draught beer, but drawn through pipes running from pub cellar to bar, by means of a piston pump system. It may also be served using a tap inserted directly into the cask. Often also called real ale.

**craft beer**  A term that originated in the USA and which meant beer produced by the small, independent breweries founded since the late 1970s – as opposed to mass-produced lagers. Now used far beyond the USA. Usually (but not exclusively) denotes beer in the style of, or inspired by, American craft brewers. Confusingly, it is also increasingly employed as a marketing term by larger established breweries for sub-brands (some of which are made using separate, smaller brewing facilities) to give the impression of being an independent brewery. The definition of craft beer is contentious, especially in the UK, but many beer enthusiasts see it as being about the ethos and intent of the brewer, especially one dedicated to making beer that puts quality before market share.

**Gueuze**  A blend of Lambic beers of different ages, typically a Lambic of two years with younger examples of up to a year.

**Helles**  A pale lager associated with Bavaria. German for 'light' or 'bright', a Helles beer is medium-bodied and of moderate strength.

**keg** (n.)  A container for beer to be served in a bar, usually made of aluminium, but sometimes plastic. The beer in a keg is usually pressurized with and dispensed by carbon dioxide, sometimes mixed with nitrogen. (adj.) Denoting beer dispensed from a keg.

**Kölsch**  Golden, fruity and moderately hoppy beer of around 4–5% ABV, originating from Cologne (Köln), Germany, where traditions of warm fermentation were kept in order to rival pale lagers.

**lite beer**  Chiefly US term denoting beer that is either low in alcohol (2% ABV or less), or lower (lighter) in carbohydrates than standard beers.

**Märzenbier** A lager traditionally brewed in March (*März* in German) before the once-decreed brewing close season that lasted from 23 April to 29 September. Brewed stronger than is standard to keep better until brewing was permitted again.

**microbrewery** A small brewery that sells almost all its beer off the premises. What constitutes 'small' is open for debate and may vary between countries. A brewery with a capacity of 10,000 hectolitres might be considered 'micro' in the USA, but regional elsewhere.

**Rauchbier** German for 'smoke beer'. Rauchbiers are usually medium-strength lagers and all contain a proportion of smoked malt. Traditionally associated with Franconia in Germany.

**real ale** Also known as cask ale, a term coined by UK consumer group CAMRA (the Campaign for Real Ale). Real ale undergoes the final stages of its maturation in a container – a cask – without having been pasteurized and with little or no filtration. As live yeast remains, the beer continues to ferment slowly, providing a light, natural carbonation when served. To conform to the definition, the beer must undergo this secondary fermentation in the vessel from which it is served and cannot be dispensed using carbon dioxide (or another gas). Similarly produced beer matured in a bottle can also be real ale.

**wheat beer** A beer made with a proportion of malted wheat as well as malted barley. Weissbier (or Weizenbier), the classic German wheat beer originating from Bavaria, contains at least 50–70% wheat. Belgian-style witbier usually contains 30–40% wheat. The 'Weiss-' and 'wit-' parts of the names of these styles mean 'white', referring to the whiteish cloudiness of the beers when they are unfiltered.

# GREAT BRITAIN

## the 30-second beer

**Beer in Britain is traditionally** drunk in pubs, and the British pub remains unique compared to bars in other countries: more inclusive and democratic, a community hub rather than a mere drinking shop, and one of Britain's most popular attractions for foreign tourists. From the late nineteenth century, most pubs were 'tied' to breweries, selling one brewery's beers exclusively. This relationship was one reason lager didn't establish a meaningful foothold in Britain when it swept the rest of the world, and British drinkers continued to prefer ale. But in the 1960s, European lager brewers signed deals with British brewers and invested heavily in marketing. During the 1970s and 1980s, Britain began drinking lager like everywhere else. In 1971 drinkers resisted the rise of lager and pasteurized 'keg' ales by forming the Campaign for Real Ale (CAMRA). Traditional British ales are live and condition in the cask, making them more variable, but also giving extra complexity and depth. Cask or 'real' ale remains an important niche product. Most pubs are no longer tied to breweries and are in decline, but still remain a totemic symbol of British life. The twenty-first century has seen an astonishing resurgence in the number of small breweries. Increasingly these new breweries embrace the global 'craft' approach, but most of their volume still consists of traditional cask ale.

**RELATED ENTRIES**
See also
ORIGINS OF MODERN ALES
page 40

BEER CHAMPIONS
page 152

**3-SECOND BIOGRAPHY**
GEORGE ORWELL
1903–50
Known mostly for novels such as *1984* and *Animal Farm*, Orwell also wrote wonderfully about beer and the British pub. His 1946 essay 'The Moon Under Water' describes his perfect pub, and still rings true today

**30-SECOND TEXT**
Pete Brown

**3-SECOND TASTER**
Britain is home to one of the world's most celebrated brewing and beer-drinking traditions, which has the traditional British pub at its heart.

**3-MINUTE BREW**
Strangely, many British drinkers tend to think foreign beers are better than British – whether this is mainstream lager with a European heritage, or US-style craft beer (British craft brewers now use more American hops than British ones.) Traditional cask ale is seen by many craft drinkers as a boring, old-fashioned product. However, the American craft brewers they revere often cite British cask ale as their inspiration, and a style they still aspire to.

*Pubs and beer, particularly cask ale, are thoroughly embedded in British culture – even George Orwell wrote about them!*

# BELGIUM

## the 30-second beer

For many years, Belgium hid its beer light under a bushel, quietly carrying on its centuries-old traditions, with beer being a part of life, art and religion. Even aside from its once-endangered cornucopia of beer styles, many famously produced by monastic brewers, there is plenty to mark Belgium out as a great beer nation. Café culture is centred on beer. The number of beer-serving establishments per head dwarfs just about everywhere. An 'ordinary' café might serve a dozen different beers, but the beer list of a top establishment can run into hundreds, with each served in glassware appropriate not just to the beer's style but also bearing the marque of the brewery from which it came. Food and beer are accepted partners both in the kitchen and at the table. The celebrated *moules frites* (mussels and fries) are served with beer – perhaps a Belgian 'white' wheat beer or a glass of 'sour' Gueuze. And that's just for starters. National dishes include Carbonade Flamande: a beef beer stew made with the Flemish *oud bruin* (old brown) style. Belgium is also the progenitor of the world's largest beer company, AB InBev, which emerged from Interbrew, Belgian owners of the ubiquitous Stella Artois lager. This Goliath was almost the downfall of the myriad of Belgium's David-sized breweries.

**RELATED ENTRIES**
See also
MONASTIC BREWERS
page 22

BELGIAN STYLES
page 80

**3-SECOND BIOGRAPHIES**
ST ARNOLD OF SOISSONS
c. 1040–87
Patron saint of hop pickers and Belgian brewers. Founded the Benedictine abbey of St Peter's of Oudenburg, West Flanders. Reportedly encouraged villagers in the time of plague to drink beer instead of contaminated water

DUKE JEAN I
c. 1251–95
Ruler of the regions now comprising Belgium, one of the historical figures that is supposedly Gambrinus, legendary 'King of Beer'

**30-SECOND TEXT**
Jerry Bartlett

*The rest of the world is catching up to what has been important in Belgian beer culture for centuries.*

**3-SECOND TASTER**
Beer culture in Belgium is deeply ingrained, with large numbers of cafes serving a diverse range of beers, and where beer naturally partners food.

**3-MINUTE BREW**
The diversity of beers in Belgium has a lot to do with its political and cultural history. Only a sovereign state since 1831, Belgium is an amalgam of two cultural halves: French-speaking Wallonia, to the south, close to wine-making France, and Dutch-speaking Flemish Flanders, which touches the great cereal belts to the north and east. This is reflected in the cross-fertilization of wine and beer cultures, with beer especially borrowing methods from wine maturation.

# GERMANY

## the 30-second beer

Germany is one of the world's greatest brewing nations. It has a record of making and drinking more beer than almost anywhere else. No surprise then that it has a long, rich beery history. Monastic brewing started here in the sixth century; Roman invaders found early Germans making 'grain wine' and archaeological finds indicate brewing took place as early as 800 BCE. Although it has many regional beers, such as the seemingly lager-like Kölsch from Cologne and strong, dark bock first brewed in Einbeck, probably the most famous – and delightful – beers are from Bavaria in southern Germany. It's home to the famous Munich Oktoberfest, actually held in September, serving amber-coloured Märzenbiers – lagers with a bready character made with speciality malts. You'll also find wheat beers served in vase-like glassware, making the most of the banana and clove aromas created by its yeast. Bamberg, in the north of the region, is famed for its Rauchbier – made with malt smoked over beechwood chips. Throughout the region the go-to lager is Helles – a soft, golden brew typically with floral hops. Modern Germans might be more likely to drink at home than their forebears, but the country is still justly famed for its beer halls and beer gardens. With their long tables and benches, they are testament to the power of beer to bring people together.

**RELATED ENTRIES**
See also
JOSEF GROLL
page 38

LAGERS
page 76

WHEAT BEERS
page 82

**3-SECOND BIOGRAPHY**
GEORG SCHNEIDER I
1817–90
Founder of the Schneider Weisse Brewery, without whom Bavaria might not be so famous for 'weissbier' today. Although the original brewery was destroyed in the Second World War and relocated to Kelheim, the family still makes wheat beer today

**30-SECOND TEXT**
Sophie Atherton

**3-SECOND TASTER**
With a long history of brewing, Germany is one of the world's true beer destinations, and Bavaria is probably its most famous brewing region.

**3-MINUTE BREW**
Germany has a famous beer purity law called the *Reinheitsgebot*. Introduced in 1516 by Duke Wilhelm IV, it restricted beer to three ingredients: barley, hops and water. Yeast was only included once its role in fermentation was understood. There's also an exception for wheat, provided beer is made with top fermenting yeast. It originally applied only to Bavaria, but when the region became part of the German Empire in 1906 it demanded the law apply to the whole country.

*Germany has a tremendous brewing history and heritage and is still a great place to explore and enjoy beer today.*

# THE REST OF EUROPE

## the 30-second beer

**3-SECOND TASTER**
Europe has a magnificent beer heritage that has only been enhanced by the craft brewing movement, and traditional wine countries are now on board, too.

**3-MINUTE BREW**
Agostino Arioli and Teo Musso are the godfathers of the Italian brewing revolution. In 1996, Arioli opened Birrificio Italiano north of Milan and began brewing distinctive beers that showed Italian drinkers what might be possible in a country that, until that point, had no small breweries. In the same year, near Turin, Musso set up Baladin and began experimenting with new ways of producing beer, creating high-end products that could compete with Italy's winemakers.

**In Europe, the national drink** tends to be defined by climate and agriculture. Southern countries where grapes are grown favour wine, while central and northern countries where barley is cultivated largely go for beer. But things are changing, and fast. The Czech Republic is famous for its beer culture. Its people drink more beer per head than any other nationality and it has made its mark on the international beer scene as the birthplace of pilsner. But not all beers here are pale; there is also a tradition of dark lagers, and now, with the arrival of new brewers, ale is becoming popular, too. Further east, Lithuania, Latvia and Estonia have long been beer-drinking nations and, emerging from Soviet control, now feature a growing craft industry, too. The Netherlands shares an affinity for beer with its two neighbours, Germany and Belgium, historically brewing pale lagers inspired by the former and potent, complex ales by the latter, but, like other countries, is also now branching out. Further south, Mediterranean wine countries are no longer good-beer deserts. In Greece, Spain and Portugal the craft scene is growing apace but it is most remarkable in Italy where there are now nearly 800 small producers. Here adventurous brewers compete with the wine industry head-on, often producing shapely, large bottles for the restaurant market.

**RELATED ENTRIES**
See also
BEER & THE INDUSTRIAL REVOLUTION
page 36

JOSEF GROLL
page 38

**3-SECOND BIOGRAPHIES**
ALFRED HENRY HEINEKEN
1923–2002
Skilfully marketed his family's business internationally, turning the Dutch beer Heineken into a global brand

AGOSTINO ARIOLI
1965–
Respected Italian brewer who proved that small breweries could succeed in a wine-dominated country

TEO MUSSO
1964–
Figurehead of the craft brewing movement in Italy, whose creative input has helped beer compete with wine

**30-SECOND TEXT**
Jeff Evans

*Beer is spreading out across Europe far beyond its traditional strongholds.*

**27 March 1942**
Born in Wetherby, Yorkshire. His family moves after the war to Leeds. Jackson trains as a journalist on the *Huddersfield Examiner*

**1976**
Writes *The English Pub*, which launches his career as a beer writer

**1977**
*The World Guide to Beer* is published and is translated into 10 languages

**1988**
Becomes the first chairman of the British Guild of Beer Writers

**1989**
Publishes *Malt Whisky*; it becomes the best-selling book on the subject

**1990**
*The Beer Hunter* TV series is shown in 15 countries

**1991**
First of five editions of the *Great Beers of Belgium* appears

**1993**
Publishes *The Beer Companion*

**2006**
Wins prestigious James Beard Award in the USA

**30 August 2007**
Dies in London

**2008**
The British Guild of Beer Writers' top prize is renamed the Michael Jackson Beer Writer of the Year Award

# MICHAEL JACKSON

Michael Jackson was the sage of beer. His books, journalism and broadcasting brought people's attention to the vast treasure trove of beers throughout the world. His greatest achievement was to prove there was far more to beer than just a pint of bitter or a glass of lager. He turned the spotlight on styles, unravelling such hidden delights as the 'wild fermentation' Lambic beers of Belgium, the history and character of a true pilsner, and the strong bock beers of Bavaria. Jackson was the first writer to pinpoint the aromas and flavours that different malts and hops give to beer. He was an inspirational force. He described Belgian beers 'as the country's best-kept secret' and through his tireless work he turned them into classic brews admired and replicated worldwide. Jackson was a 'frequent flyer', repeatedly crossing the Atlantic to encourage the beer revolution there. He endlessly toured that vast continent, visiting many of the pioneers of craft beer and recording their efforts to counter the giant brewers and their insipid brews.

Jackson was born in Yorkshire but lived for many years in London. He was descended from Lithuanian Jews; his father Anglicized his name from Isaac Jakowitz to Jack Jackson and gave his son a name that would cause amusement in later years with the rise of the singer Michael Jackson. Jackson trained as a journalist in Yorkshire and went on to work on newspapers and magazines in Edinburgh and London. It was a background that introduced him to the pleasures of beer and pubs. He had a lucky break in 1976: a writer had failed to deliver a book on the English pub and Jackson was asked to take over. The experience could have encouraged him to concentrate on British beer but he set his sights higher. A year later he published the seminal *World Guide to Beer* that made his name. It was translated into 10 languages and transformed drinkers' knowledge of beer.

In 1990 Jackson turned from print to film with the TV series *The Beer Hunter*. It was seen in 15 countries and brought to an even wider audience his passion for the great beers of Europe and the USA. More books followed, including seven editions of his *Pocket Beer Book* and five editions of the *Great Beers of Belgium*. In total he sold three million books.

Jackson suffered with Parkinson's disease, which triggered a fatal heart attack in 2007. A decade later, his work and inspiration live on wherever good beer is enjoyed.

*Roger Protz*

# UNITED STATES
## the 30-second beer

**3-SECOND TASTER**
American beer long had
a reputation for being the
world's blandest – until
the craft beer revolution
took it back in the
opposite direction.

**3-MINUTE BREW**
American craft beer is
so exciting because it is
a reaction against the
total disappearance of
flavourful, characterful
beer. In renowned brewing
countries such as Britain,
Germany, Belgium and the
Czech Republic, the desire
to innovate is always
counterbalanced by the
preservation of a national
brewing tradition. In the
USA, there was no tradition
left to preserve, so craft
brewers were free to take
inspiration from all those
countries to create
something new.

**Almost a hundred years on, beer**
in the United States is still shaped by Prohibition.
Between 1920 and 1933, it was illegal to sell or
distribute alcohol. When Prohibition ended,
few of America's brewers had survived, and the
public had lost the taste for the German-style
lagers they had enjoyed since the 1870s.
American beer became substantially lighter
in taste. In the 1970s, the 'Beer Wars' saw
Anheuser Busch, Miller and Coors try to destroy
each other with aggressive marketing campaigns
and new product launches. Each survived and
grew much bigger, but hundreds of smaller
breweries were put out of business. Three
brands, Budweiser, Miller and Coors, accounted
for over 80% of the market, with 'Lite' beers
that were virtually indistinguishable from
each other. And then, in 1979, the Carter
administration got rid of Prohibition's final
hangover: a ban on homebrewing that had
remained in place due to administrative
oversight. America's homebrewers began
creating beers influenced by British, German
and Belgian styles, and the best quickly turned
pro: the craft brewing movement was born. The
big brands still dominate, but craft is consistently
stealing share from them. American-style craft
beers, particularly those brewed with American
hops, are the dominant influence on the
emerging global craft beer movement.

**RELATED ENTRIES**
See also
AMERICAN CRAFT BEERS
page 86

CORPORATE BREWING
page 118

**3-SECOND BIOGRAPHIES**
ADOLPHUS BUSCH
1839–1913
German-American who, along
with his father-in-law Eberhard
Anheuser, founded the brewery
that launched Budweiser,
America's biggest-selling beer

FRITZ MAYTAG
1937–
The heir of the massive Maytag
kitchen appliance company,
Maytag bought San Francisco's
ailing Anchor Brewing Company
in 1965 and turned it into
what is now widely regarded
as America's first modern
craft brewery

**30-SECOND TEXT**
Pete Brown

*Don't be fooled into
thinking American beer
means light lager and
little else; the USA is a
prime mover in the craft
beer revolution.*

# SCANDINAVIA

## the 30-second beer

### 3-SECOND TASTER
In 25 years, the Scandic beer scene has transformed from a monoculture dominated by German styles to a duoculture dominated by American craft styles – and Carlsberg.

### 3-MINUTE BREW
For Scandinavians, beer is part of the culture. Each brewery produces its own Easter and Christmas beers to go with the celebratory dinner. The smörgåsbord at Midsummer includes beer as accompaniment alongside flavoured vodka. A 'funeral beer' is solace when anything needs putting to rest. Scandinavia kept Baltic porter alive and now makes world-class imperial stouts (Lervig), sours (Brekeriet) and beers that challenge what we think a beer can be (Omnipollo and Mikkeller).

### Beer culture in Scandinavia

is deeply ingrained. Beer is an accepted accompaniment to seasonal celebrations and as a drink for all classes and genders. Until recently, the market consisted of Carlsberg and a few large regional breweries, which had gradually assimilated local breweries. Choice began to improve in the 1990s as microbreweries and brewpubs started popping up. Then in 2006, Mikkeller happened. Two Danish homebrewers turned pro, eventually producing a huge variety of beers despite not having their own brewery. Mikkeller acquired a stellar reputation and inspired a new generation of Scandinavians to return to brewing local and small. From a few dozen breweries in 1996, by the end of 2017 there were hundreds, with Sweden alone accounting for 300. The farmhouse brewing gene that hadn't quite been eradicated in Gotland in the Baltic and the fjords of Norway, found new life. Even so, beer for most people still means standard lager. However, the widespread love of British and US pub culture is making people more adventurous. On top of this, a tolerance for prices that non-Scandis find eye-watering means new breweries must quickly come up to standard, or be ditched. Now, like a second wave of Vikings, expect to find more Scandinavian beers near you – and not just the blondes.

### RELATED ENTRY
See also
HOMEBREWING
page 122

### 3-SECOND BIOGRAPHIES
JACOB CHRISTIAN JACOBSEN
1811–87
Philanthropic Danish founder of Carlsberg in 1847; creator of first brewery-owned research laboratory, from where Emil Christian Hansen developed the single-strain lager yeast, *Saccharomyces carlsbergensis*

MIKKEL BORG BJERGSØ
1975–
Danish former homebrewer and teacher, who with Kristian Klarup Keller founded Mikkeller. Physically investing in brewing beers by renting space in other breweries, Bjergsø went solo, providing the catalyst to microbreweries across the region

### 30-SECOND TEXT
Jerry Bartlett

*Scandinavian breweries are returning to small, local and creative beers, often with classy designs.*

# ASIA & AFRICA

## the 30-second beer

For decades, Asia and Africa have been significant beer producers but most of the output has been pale lager; in Asia, rice features strongly in the recipes. This gives many local beers a crispness and lightness of body, but many drinkers are now seeking beers with deeper character. China is the world's largest beer producer and the country is now breaking out of its shell – at least in metropolitan areas where brewpubs have arrived – to offer more exciting products. They may be inspired by the substantial craft brewing movement in Japan, where brewers such as Kiuchi (Hitachino Nest) and Minoh are already well known to the international cognoscenti. The same is happening in Taiwan, South Korea, Vietnam and also in India, where beer has never been hugely popular. In sun-baked Africa, while many countries major on quenching lagers, Nigeria has been home to one of the largest Guinness breweries since the 1960s, proving that local drinkers also have a taste for stout. Tusker from Kenya and Windhoek from Namibia are well-known lager brands but it is in South Africa that artisan production is now really taking off, with companies such as Devil's Peak and Anvil Ale House winning awards in international competitions.

**RELATED ENTRIES**
See also
THE ORIGINS OF BEER
page 30

ARTHUR GUINNESS
page 78

**3-SECOND TASTER**
The continents of Asia and Africa, as they break away from tradition, are rapidly becoming areas of interest for the beer drinker.

**3-MINUTE BREW**
The use of rice in Asia is typical of the way in which brewers over centuries have included locally grown crops in their beers. In Africa, too, there is evidence of this, with sorghum and maize both featuring in traditional, small-scale beer production, particularly to create the cloudy brew called Chibuku, although the increased availability of barley and the spread of industrialization have seen the development of a beer culture more familiar to the outside world.

**3-SECOND BIOGRAPHIES**
KIUCHI GIHEI
1795–unknown
The headman of a Japanese village who founded a sake brewery in 1823 that began producing Hitachino Nest craft beer in 1996

LEX MITCHELL
1950–
Former South African Breweries employee who set up his own small Mitchells Brewery in Knysna, South Africa, in 1983, well ahead of the craft beer revolution. He is now a brewmaster with Bridge Street Brewery in Port Elizabeth

**30-SECOND TEXT**
Jeff Evans

*Although lager is dominant across Asia and Africa, there's also growing interest in craft beer and a love of stout.*

# SOUTHERN HEMISPHERE

## the 30-second beer

If you believe the television commercials, beer in Australia is all about golden lagers drunk by macho guys with a questionable sense of humour. The reality is somewhat different. While major brands still dominate, the country is home to a booming craft brewing movement. Arguably, this began in the 1860s, with the founding of Cooper's, an Adelaide company known for its Sparkling Ale, but, in modern times, one of the biggest names to emerge was Little Creatures. There have been hundreds of exciting breweries since. Many, such as Hawthorn, Hawkers, Prancing Pony and Edge Brewing Project, are now international award winners. New Zealand is equally well endowed with high-quality brewers, some of which – Tuatara, 8 Wired and Yeastie Boys – market their beers internationally as the New Zealand Brewing Collective. Australia and New Zealand are also noted for their own hop varieties that offer bold floral and tropical fruit notes. Elsewhere, a fascinating development has been the unfolding brewing scene in South America. Peru, Chile and Argentina are rapidly jumping aboard the beer bandwagon but Brazil is really forging ahead. It all started with companies such as DaDoBier, Colorado and Baden Baden in the 1990s but now there are adventurous small breweries all over this huge country.

**RELATED ENTRIES**
See also
HOPS
page 54

SPECIALITY BREWING
page 64

**3-SECOND TASTER**
Proving that the beer revolution is sweeping the world, countries in the southern hemisphere are just as dynamic, skilful and ambitious as their northern counterparts.

**3-MINUTE BREW**
In Brazil, areas that enjoy a German heritage – the legacies of migrants past – have given rise to breweries such as Baden Baden and Eisenbahn. German styles feature in their ranges but so do beers inspired by American craft brewing and other international cultures. Brazil is also looking inward, reaping the harvest of the Amazon rainforest to produce stunning beers aged in tropical hardwood, for instance, or laced with unusual tropical fruits and herbs.

**3-SECOND BIOGRAPHIES**
THOMAS COOPER
1826–97
Founded one of Australia's oldest and best-known breweries in 1862

MARCELO CARNEIRO
1960–
One of Brazil's brewing pioneers, founding Colorado Brewery in 1996 and featuring indigenous South American ingredients in his beers

JULIANO MENDES
1975–
Brazilian brewer and food producer who co-founded Eisenbahn in 2002

**30-SECOND TEXT**
Jeff Evans

*It's not just tinnies for the barbie; the Southern Hemisphere boasts a growing craft beer scene.*

# CRAFT BEER AROUND THE WORLD

## the 30-second beer

**As the twentieth century turned** into the twenty-first, the beer world began to change. The USA and the UK were the prime movers in this craft beer revolution, but the idea of brewing something other than the prevalent or local style, or beginning to make beer in countries dominated by wine, has taken off in a surprising number of places around the globe. A couple of hot spots not covered in the preceding pages are Ireland and Canada. Guinness, and to an extent lager, still dominate the island of Ireland but both the Republic and Northern Ireland are enjoying an increase in the number of breweries and a growing craft beer scene. Ten to 15 years ago there were only a handful of breweries; now there are more than 100. Canada's craft beer scene is rich and varied, with different European influences depending on where you look. Numbers of small independent breweries have been slowly increasing since the 1980s, then rose dramatically soon after the start of the twenty-first century. There were fewer than 100; now there are more than 500. It's also one of the few places outside the UK with an interest in real ale – since 2005 Toronto has been home to annual festival Cask Days. Almost anywhere in the world where alcohol is legal, these days there's a chance of finding a microbrewery or brewpub.

**RELATED ENTRIES**
See also
PACKAGING & DISPENSE
page 24

THE ORIGINS OF BEER
page 30

ARTHUR GUINNESS
page 78

**30-SECOND TEXT**
Sophie Atherton

**3-SECOND TASTER**
Beer has always been a geographically widespread drink, but since the turn of the century local craft brewing scenes have emerged in more and more places.

**3-MINUTE BREW**
Even France has developed a thirst for craft beer, or *la bière artisanale*. There are hundreds of microbreweries and brewpubs making a wide variety of traditional and modern beer styles. Historically, French breweries were mostly found in rural locations and made beer for the nearby community. Now cities and towns are home to great French beer. Paris has a thriving scene, including its own annual beer week, and smaller cities like Lyon are not far behind.

*The idea of craft beer, and the movement surrounding it, has seen brewing expand in exciting ways throughout the world.*

# THE BEER INDUSTRY

**beer garden** Garden or outdoor area of a pub, especially in the UK, used as area to drink and eat. (Equivalent to *Biergarten* in Germany.)

**beer hall** A large pub where the predominant beverage served is beer. Beer halls are commonly associated with Germany.

**craft beer** A term that originated in the USA and which meant beer produced by the small, independent breweries founded since the late 1970s – as opposed to mass-produced lagers. Now used far beyond the USA. Usually (but not exclusively) denotes beer in the style of, or inspired by, American craft brewers. Confusingly, it is also increasingly employed as a marketing term by larger established breweries for sub-brands (some of which are made using separate, smaller brewing facilities) to give the impression of being an independent brewery. The definition of craft beer is contentious, especially in the UK, but many beer enthusiasts see it as being about the ethos and intent of the brewer, especially one dedicated to making beer that puts quality before market share.

*cuisine à la bière* French term for a style of cooking, not limited to French or Belgian, that gives prominence to beer as an ingredient.

**Industrial Revolution** The rapid development of industry that began in Britain in the late eighteenth century, brought about by the introduction of machinery.

**malt extract** A syrup or powder derived from malted barley containing the fermentable sugars required for brewing. Mainly used by homebrewers to simplify the brewing process by replacing or supplementing malted grains.

**Märzen** A lager traditionally brewed in March (*März* in German) before the once-decreed brewing close season that lasted from 23 April to 29 September. Brewed stronger than is standard to keep better until brewing was permitted again.

**Oktoberfest** The largest beer festival in Germany, and probably the world, is part of a fayre, which takes place in Munich every year. Lasting 16 to 18 days, depending on the calendar, it ends on the first weekend in October and so is often mostly in September. Beer is served in large tents or marquees seating thousands of guests and is supplied only by the half-dozen large breweries situated within Munich's boundaries.

**one-vessel brewing**  A beer-brewing system that consists of a single container in which all the stages of the beer-making process take place, as opposed to the traditional system that uses three separate containers for the distinct stages.

**pubco**  A pub company, that is, a company set up to own and run a chain of pubs, without owning any brewery that supplies beer to its pubs. The company leases the pub to be run by tenants/licensees rather than employees. Beer is sold by the pubco at fixed prices to its pubs. The practice is widespread in the UK.

**real ale**  Also known as cask ale, a term coined by UK consumer group CAMRA (the Campaign for Real Ale). Real ale undergoes the final stages of its maturation in a container – a cask – without having been pasteurized and with little or no filtration. As live yeast remains, the beer continues to ferment slowly, providing a light, natural carbonation when served. To conform to the definition, the beer must undergo this secondary fermentation in the vessel from which it is served and cannot be dispensed using carbon dioxide (or other gas). Similarly produced beer matured in a bottle can also be real ale.

**stein**  Glazed, kilned stoneware drinking vessel traditionally used to serve beer in Germany. Derives from 'stone' in German.

**taproom**  A bar either in or close to a brewery, that predominantly serves the beers brewed by that brewery.

# CORPORATE BREWING

## the 30-second beer

**For most of its history, brewing** was small-scale and highly localized. The Industrial Revolution allowed brewers with money and vision to grow rapidly, but they still mostly dominated their local areas. Then, in the late nineteenth century, rail travel and refrigeration allowed a big brewer to potentially sell its beer across the world, and the biggest companies floated on the stock market to fund further expansion. The twentieth century saw a long, gradual decline in beer consumption in mature western markets. Big brewers were obliged to keep corporate shareholders happy by delivering ever-better returns. The only ways to do this in a shrinking market were: reduce costs, take share from the competition, or acquire that competition by merger or takeover. Beers became blander so they would offend no one. Investment went into marketing to create powerful brands but cost-cutting meant beer was commoditized and distinctions between big brands disappeared. The early twenty-first century therefore saw a rapid consolidation of brewers operating in a global market, with fewer names dominating more territories. The world's biggest brewer, Anheuser Busch, now controls a third of the entire world's beer supply. Together with Molson Coors, Heineken, Carlsberg and Diageo, a handful of companies now own more than 90% of the world's beer.

**RELATED ENTRIES**
See also
UNITED STATES
page 104

CRAFT BEER
page 120

**3-SECOND BIOGRAPHY**
CARLOS BRITO
1960–
Brazilian businessman who oversaw a series of mergers and acquisitions that saw Brazilian brewer Brahma become Ambev, then Inbev, then Anheuser-Busch Inbev (AB-Inbev), the world's biggest brewer; he focuses on delivering higher returns through a programme of relentless cost-cutting

**30-SECOND TEXT**
Pete Brown

**3-SECOND TASTER**
Most of the world's beer is owned by five companies, all trying to deliver ever-increasing growth from a market that's in long-term volume decline.

**3-MINUTE BREW**
Interest in craft beer is, in part, a reaction against corporate hegemony, driven by a desire to support small businesses as much as a yearning for flavourful, interesting beer. But big corporations are inevitably acquiring craft brewers to attempt to control this small but rapidly growing sector of the market. Such acquisitions are met with howls of outrage from the craft beer community – but corporates facing ever-intensifying pressure wouldn't be doing their jobs if they ignored craft.

*Despite the advent of craft brewing, 90% of the world's beer is still owned by just a handful of multinational companies.*

# CRAFT BEER

## the 30-second beer

The beer world was turned upside down in the twenty-first century as a result of the craft revolution – driven by young brewers with passion and zeal, partly inspired by small-batch food producers who value provenance and the finest natural ingredients. Craft beer, too, is centred on beers the brewers themselves want to drink, using the best malts and hops, in sharp contrast to the cheap ingredients used by global producers. The thrust of the craft beer movement comes from the USA and UK. The UK has a long tradition of making beer slowly and naturally – best illustrated by cask-conditioned beer (or real ale), which is neither filtered nor pasteurized. CAMRA saved cask beer, paving the way for the growth of new small breweries, of which there are now some 2,000 in Britain. In the USA, the growth of craft is fuelled by consumer opposition to the bland products of global giants. There are now more than 5,000 American craft breweries producing an amazing range of beers. There are close to 800 small breweries in Italy, and craft production is growing in such countries as China, Hungary and Japan. Down Under, there are close to 400 small independents in Australia and 150 in New Zealand. There is no slowing down in the demand for craft, which is now a worldwide phenomenon.

### 3-SECOND TASTER
The buzz word of the beer world is 'craft' – thousands of brewers have sprung up to offer greater choice to drinkers and challenge the power of global giants.

### 3-MINUTE BREW
In the USA, the Brewers Association, which speaks for the independent sector, defines a craft brewer as one producing up to six million barrels a year and must be no more than 25% owned by a company that is itself not a craft brewer. There is no such definition in the UK but the term may be taken to mean an independent brewer that pays lower rates of duty under the government's Small Brewers Relief scheme.

### RELATED ENTRY
See also
BEER CHAMPIONS
page 152

### 3-SECOND BIOGRAPHY
BERT GRANT
1928–2001
A key player in the American craft beer movement. In 1982 he established the first US brewpub since Prohibition in Yakima Valley, Washington State. He upgraded to a full brewery in 1990, producing pale ale, IPA, Scots Ale and stout and helping to highlight the potential of Pacific Northwest hops

### 30-SECOND TEXT
Roger Protz

*Craft beer emerged from a desire to make and drink more flavoursome brews than those already available.*

CAMRA

CAMPAIGN
FOR
REAL ALE

# HOMEBREWING

## the 30-second beer

Before the Industrial Revolution, homebrewing was where most beer came from. After, almost nobody homebrewed, either for legal reasons, or because they were too busy working at the mill. It was legalized in the UK in 1963, but the homebrew produced was often poor quality. Legalization in the USA in 1979 turned out differently, effectively kick-starting the American craft beer movement that inspired the world. Superstar brewers Ken Grossman (Sierra Nevada), Denmark's Mikkel Borg Bjergsø (Mikkeller), Australian David Hollyoak (Redoak) and many others, all started as homebrewers. Now, homebrewing is popular almost everywhere beer is. In 2017 in the USA, an estimated 1.1 million homebrewers made 1.7 million barrels of homebrew. The hobby is supported by a worldwide homebrew supplies industry, with online and local shops providing a vast range of equipment and ingredients. The market in the UK is worth around £25m. A homebrewer's path can easily go from a stove-top beginner, brewing from a couple of cans of malt extract, to advanced, brewing sophisticated recipes with exotic malts, hops, yeast and other boundary-pushing ingredients. Even if you don't intend to go pro, and just want to impress your friends with an authentic Märzen lager for your own Oktoberfest, your homebrewed beer can rival the quality of commercial beers, not just the price.

**RELATED ENTRIES**
See also
BEER IN THE TWENTIETH CENTURY
page 42

HOW BEER IS MADE
page 48

**3-SECOND BIOGRAPHIES**
DAVE LINE
1942–80
Pioneering British writer of homebrewing books, such as *Brewing Beers Like Those You Buy*. Influenced a generation of homebrewers and writers, helping make homebrewing respectable

ANDY HAMILTON
1974–
British author, broadcaster and industry adviser on homebrewing and a wide range of drinks-related subjects, often making use of wild or home-grown ingredients.

**30-SECOND TEXT**
Jerry Bartlett

*Once the province of the bootlegger or cheapskate, homebrewing can produce seriously good beers.*

**3-SECOND TASTER**
Homebrewing has progressed beyond a way of making cheap beer – professional-quality beer is possible and many commercial brewers hone their skills before turning pro.

**3-MINUTE BREW**
A malt extract kit is the homebrewer's typical starting point. The malt comes pre-processed into a concentrate with added hop extract. Stepping up to doing an all-grain full mash needs more equipment and work, but gives freedom of choice over malts and hops. Serious hobbyists might progress to a one-vessel brewing system, which does the mash and the boil. Add a mini-fermenter and you have a professional kit for a couple of grand.

# TRADE ORGANIZATIONS

## the 30-second beer

There are so many important issues related to the business of brewing – from taxation and licensing laws to environmental matters and the health lobby – that there is a clear logic in brewers banding together to fight their corner. In the USA, the body that helps promote the work of brewers and challenges legislators is the Brewers Association, which also stages the Great American Beer Festival and has played a fundamental part in the remarkable growth of the American craft brewing sector. In the UK, there are two organizations that fulfil this role. The British Beer & Pub Association (BBPA) largely represents the biggest breweries along with long-established regionals, while the Society of Independent Brewers (SIBA) provides a voice for most of the smaller concerns. Similar associations are in place around the world, including the Brewers Association of Australia, Unionbirrai in Italy and the Brewers Association of Japan. The over-arching Brewers of Europe brings together 26 member bodies from within the EU, plus three associate members, to work on a supranational level. Related industries also have representative bodies, like the Maltsters' Association of Great Britain and Hop Growers of America, as do pubs and bars, with the Association of Licensed Multiple Retailers (now UK Hospitality) and the British Institute of Innkeeping prominent in the UK.

**3-SECOND TASTER**
'No man is an island,' declared English poet John Donne, and the brewing industry with its numerous, important trade associations recognizes that only too well.

**3-MINUTE BREW**
Depending on their needs, some breweries belong to more than one association. The Independent Family Brewers of Britain, for instance, is a grouping of some of the country's oldest breweries that still have founding family members involved in the business. These brewers understand that such personal involvement is an asset that needs to be promoted, and also recognize that there are particular issues relevant to their shared heritage and company structures that are best addressed collectively.

**RELATED ENTRIES**
See also
GREAT BRITAIN
page 94

UNITED STATES
page 104

CRAFT BEER
page 120

BEER CHAMPIONS
page 152

**3-SECOND BIOGRAPHIES**
CHARLIE PAPAZIAN
1949–
Founder of the Association of Brewers (later the Brewers Association) and its president for 37 years, overseeing the rise of craft brewing in America

MIKE BENNER
1966–
Former chief executive of CAMRA, who became managing director of the Society of Independent Brewers in 2014

**30-SECOND TEXT**
Jeff Evans

*The brewing industry recognizes the power of collective action.*

# PUBS, BARS & BEER GARDENS

## the 30-second beer

### Beer has always been sociable.

The drink that everyone can enjoy – and afford. Whether relaxing and chatting, celebrating or commiserating, plotting or planning, pubs and bars provide the perfect setting to gather and share a pint. In Europe, while monasteries offered hospitality through the Dark and Middle Ages, inns date back to pre-Roman times. In Britain, the pub was the only place to enjoy fresh cask beer, and breweries built up vast pub estates. These morphed into pub companies (or 'pubcos'), often to the detriment of selection and quality. By contrast, a free house is unfettered in what beer it can offer. Today's threats to pubs revolve around the availability of good beer in shops, but drinking on the premises remains popular – with many types of place to do so. Often more industrial chic than cosy havens, brewery taprooms are on the rise, offering brewers the chance to serve their beers just how they want. Community and micro-pubs are also springing up. Globally, pubs and bars are the social hub of many communities. Bavaria has *gemütlichkeit*, that sense of true conviviality, and beer gardens and halls cater for thousands. While homely Czech restaurants proudly sport beer tanks, Belgium has *cuisine à la bière*. With the craft beer revolution in full swing, US bars and brewpubs are thriving, and restaurants embrace beer with a new-found confidence.

RELATED ENTRIES
See also
GREAT BRITAIN
page 94

BELGIUM
page 96

BEER & FOOD MATCHING
page 142

**3-SECOND BIOGRAPHIES**
DAVID BRUCE
1948–
Serial entrepreneur who reignited brewpub culture in the UK in late 1970s with his Firkin group of brewpubs

TIM MARTIN
1955–
Founder of UK high street pub chain J D Wetherspoon – now something of a British institution.

**30-SECOND TEXT**
Susanna Forbes

**3-SECOND TASTER**
The world over, beer has been at the heart of a thriving bar and pub culture since the beginning of time – today it's reaching the restaurant scene, too.

**3-MINUTE BREW**
While beer gardens and beer halls are popular all around the world, in Bavaria they are legendary. Beginning as spaces next to the town's lagering cellars or the brewery itself, often in the shade of gigantic, sprawling trees, they soon became an institution. Sitting at communal tables, drinkers are encouraged to bring food, even sometimes their own steins. Munich in particular embraces the outdoors, boasting 80 beer gardens, the largest of which, Hirschgarten, seats 8,000.

*Originally springing up outside breweries or a town or city's lagering cellars, Bavarian beer gardens are renowned for their spirit of enjoyment.*

**1982**
James Watt and Martin Dickie both born in Aberdeenshire, Scotland

**2004**
Dickie graduates from Heriot-Watt University with a BSc in Brewing and Distilling; Watt graduates from Edinburgh University with a degree in Law and Economics

**2005–2007**
Dickie cuts his brewing teeth at Thornbridge Brewing, Derbyshire – another of the UK's successful craft breweries

**2007**
Watt & Dickie co-found BrewDog, renting a home for their brewery in Fraserburgh about 65km (40 miles) north of Aberdeen

**2008**
Hit the headlines for their efforts to brew the world's strongest beer; win supermarket beer competition leading to BrewDog being stocked nationwide

**2009**
Launch of first Equity for Punks crowdfunding scheme, attracting more than 1,300 investors

**2010**
The first BrewDog bar opens, in Aberdeen

**2011**
Three more BrewDog bars open in Edinburgh, Glasgow and London – the last launched by Dickie and Watts hiring a tank to drive them down Camden High Street; second Equity for Punks crowdfunding bid attracts some 5,000 investors

**2012**
Move to new state-of-the-art brewery in Ellon, Aberdeenshire. Open a further six bars

**2013**
Equity for Punks III raises £4.25 million from almost 10,000 new investors; first overseas BrewDog bar opens in Sweden

**2016**
Watt and Dickie awarded MBEs in the Queen's Birthday Honours List

**2017**
Celebrate 10 years of BrewDog; open USA-based brewery in Columbus, Ohio and launch the 'Unicorn Fund' through which Watts and Dickie pledge to give away 20% of their profits every year, 10% to be shared between their employees and 10% donated to charity

# JAMES WATT & MARTIN DICKIE

**More than 30 years after punk** rock, two school friends from Aberdeenshire, James Watt and Martin Dickie, started brewing together because they couldn't find any beer they liked. As with punk music their inspiration came from the USA. They wanted to drink the sort of big, hoppy pale ales prevalent in the American craft beer scene and to do everything their own way. They came up with Punk IPA, which would become their best-selling flagship brew, and set out their stall as the punks of beer. Their approach made them as many enemies as fans, helped craft beer in the UK go mainstream and led to a stack of acolytes and accolades. They called their venture BrewDog, a name inspired by their chocolate Labrador, Bracken, and declared it a mission to spread their passion for great beer.

In keeping with their image and attitude, they decided to stick two fingers up to cask beer (aka real ale). Instead, going against the grain of the UK's brewing traditions, they made draught beer only for keg. Cooler and fizzier than cask, it was no less flavourful owing to their obsession with hops. This marked them out as villains in the eyes of many members of the important and influential British consumer group the Campaign for Real Ale (CAMRA). Using roadkill animals as beer bottle holders, driving a tank down London's Camden High Street and making the world's strongest beer were among their early marketing ploys. But what seemed a series of outlandish publicity stunts went on to become as much a part of their brand as their beer.

Yet if all they were known for was bragging and making a show of themselves, they wouldn't be as successful as they are. The most important thing about BrewDog is making great beer – thanks in no small part to investment in quality control and obsessive attention to detail. It helped them become pioneers of beer industry crowdfunding, with five incarnations of their Equity for Punks scheme attracting tens of thousands of investors. It also enabled them to develop a chain of bars in the UK, Europe and beyond, offering top-notch customer service and staff beer knowledge.

When it comes to punk street cred they might be more Malcolm McLaren than Ramones, but there's no denying BrewDog's role in the craft beer revolution and influence on the UK beer scene.

*Sophie Atherton*

# SPECIALIST RETAILERS

## the 30-second beer

With the number of breweries rising and competition for space in pubs and bars increasingly tough, brewers have turned to the bottle and can as a means of finding a way to market. This in turn has developed a new retailing sector – the speciality beer outlet, the growth of which is well illustrated by the experience in the UK. There, pioneering beer shops opened their doors in the 1970s but the idea has really taken over in recent years, with hundreds of shops now offering excellent selections of beers. This variety – combined with lower prices than in pubs and other social trends that have made home consumption more appealing – means that 'off-trade' sales – helped along by online traders and subscription clubs – now surpass 'on-trade' sales in the UK. In the USA, the position is even more advanced, with some 80% of beer sales 'off-premise', delivered by a mixture of specialist beer outlets, off-licences, supermarkets and petrol stations. In Ireland, too, the long-standing preference for pub drinking is being eroded, and the scenario is similar elsewhere in the world, as established Australian 'bottle-os' and newer dedicated venues such as Empório Alto dos Pinheiros in São Paulo, Brazil – to give just two examples – increasingly turn drinkers' heads.

## 3-SECOND TASTER
Not long ago, the choice of beers available in shops was limited – now it is astonishing, and the number of specialist outlets has rocketed.

## 3-MINUTE BREW
A by-product of the craft brewing revolution is the bottle shop and bar. The concept is simple but effective. The retailer stocks a huge range of interesting bottled and canned beers which customers can peruse while enjoying a draught beer from the bar, or a bottle from one of the fridges. With clients relaxed and having more time to choose, and the venue selling beer to them while they're deliberating, everyone's a winner.

## RELATED ENTRY
See also
PACKAGING & DISPENSE
page 24

## 3-SECOND BIOGRAPHIES
DON YOUNGER
& JOY CAMPBELL
1942–2010 & 1948–
Co-founders of Belmont Station in Portland, Oregon, in 1997 – one of the first destination beer stores in the USA. Now run by beer writer Lisa Morrison

MARTIN KEMP
1957–
Acquired the Two Brewers off-licence in London in 1982 and transformed it into a magnet called The Beer Shop that finally closed in 2005

CHRIS MENICHELLI
1986–
Set up Slow Beer in Melbourne, a pioneer among Australia's specialist retailers, in 2009

## 30-SECOND TEXT
Jeff Evans

*Shops dedicated to beer are often owned and staffed by knowledgeable enthusiasts.*

# BEER APPRECIATION

**barley wine**  An ale of British origin, usually amber to bronze in colour. Named because of its wine-like strength, around 8–12% ABV, and predominant malted barley flavour. Usually less bitter than equivalent strength IPAs.

**bottle conditioned**  Beer that continues to ferment in its bottle owing to the presence of yeast. Must be stored upright and, unless a yeasty or hazy style, poured carefully so as not to disturb the sediment.

**brewmaster**  The head brewer of a brewery.

**Champion Beer of Britain**  Title presented by CAMRA (The Campaign for Real Ale) to the British real ale adjudged best in competition at the Great British Beer Festival, an annual beer festival held in London in August. Often abbreviated to CBoB and pronounced 'see-bob'.

**Great American Beer Festival**  Three-day Beer festival held every September or October in Denver, Colorado. Founded in 1982 to showcase homebrewed beer, it is now the largest craft beer festival in America, with some 800 breweries participating.

**imperial stout**  Originally, an extra strong stout of around 10% ABV brewed by London brewers for export to the Russian Czarina, Catherine the Great, at the Russian Imperial court in the late 18th century. The style became fashionable and was copied widely before falling into decline. Interest in the style has recently been renewed, inspired by modern American brewers' interpretations. However, the meaning of 'imperial' has become vague, and is sometimes as low as 7% ABV. The term 'imperial' is now applied to other beer styles brewed to a stronger than expected strength.

**New England IPA**  A beer style that is a variation on the theme of IPA. Typically, it has strong, fruity hop aromas and lower levels of bitterness than are usually associated with American-style IPAs. This is achieved by adding large amounts of hops after the beer has fermented (dry hopping), which also gives the beer a cloudy appearance.

**nitro (stout)**  A stout (or other beer) dispensed using nitrogen under pressure, usually mixed with a much lower proportion of carbon dioxide. The beer emerges with a persistent creamy head and smooth mouthfeel (texture).

**Oktoberfest** The largest beer festival in Germany, and probably the world, is part of a fayre, which takes place in Munich every year. Beer is served in large tents or marquees seating thousands of guests and is supplied only by the half-dozen large breweries situated within Munich's boundaries.

**oxidized** Beer that has become oxidized is considered faulty. A chemical reaction, called oxidation, occurs when oxygen comes into contact with beer during brewing or storage. If not controlled or eliminated, oxidation produces undesirable stale flavours.

**real ale** Also known as cask ale, a term coined by UK consumer group CAMRA (the Campaign for Real Ale). Real ale undergoes the final stages of its maturation in a container – a cask – without having been pasteurized and with little or no filtration. As live yeast remains, the beer continues to ferment slowly, providing a light, natural carbonation when served. To conform to the definition, the beer must undergo this secondary fermentation in the vessel from which it is served and cannot be dispensed using carbon dioxide (or another gas). Similarly produced beer matured in a bottle can also be real ale.

**unfined beer** Beer made without the aid of finings, which are used to remove yeast and protein particles in the final stages of production to make beer clearer. Finings are additives usually derived from natural substances; isinglass (made from the swim bladders of fish) is commonly used. Some brewers don't add finings because it is thought that some desirable flavours and textures may be lost. Because some finings are derived from animal products an unfined beer can usually be relied upon to be suitable for vegans.

**wheat beer** An ale (usually warm fermented) made with a significant proportion of malted wheat as well as malted barley. Weissenbier (or Weizenbier), the classic German wheat beer originating from Bavaria contain at least 50–70% wheat. Belgian-style witbier usually contains 30–40% wheat. The 'Weiss-' and 'wit-' parts of the names of these styles mean 'white', referring to the whiteish cloudiness of the beers when they are unfiltered.

# HOW TO TASTE BEER

## the 30-second beer

Tasting beer is not the same as merely drinking it. Anyone can tip beer down their neck then wipe the back of their hand across their mouth, but a little thought enables you to get much more out of it. Before tasting, give your beer a sniff, just as wine lovers do. All its ingredients may contribute to aroma as well as taste, but the popularity of hoppy beers make it likely your first aromatic impression will be from hops. Whatever it's from, it should be appealing. Next take a sip and pause to consider what you can taste. What does it remind you of, does it please you, do you want more? Answering these questions will assist in forming an opinion of the beer and deciding if it's the drink for you. Take a second sip and breathe in through your nose to smell the beer at the same time. Taste and smell are inextricably linked and your perception of the beer comes from both. Additional flavours and aromas that you didn't notice at first may be apparent in the second taste. Consider also how the beer feels in your mouth – thin or full, fizzy or flat – and what sort of aftertaste is left behind. The best beers should both satisfy and also leave you wanting more.

**RELATED ENTRIES**
See also
HOW BEER IS MADE
page 48

BEER QUALITY
page 140

BEER JUDGING
page 148

**3-SECOND TASTER**
Tasting beer is the act of considering its flavour and aroma, rather than simply drinking it without understanding why you like or dislike it.

**3-MINUTE BREW**
As well as taste, flavour and aroma take time to consider a beer's appearance – including colour, clarity and head (or foam). Many should be crystal clear with no haze or particles in sight; in others haze is acceptable. Some styles, such as wheat beers, are intentionally cloudy. Brewing trends, such as unfined beer and a style known as New England IPA, have muddied the waters about whether murky beer is appropriate or desirable.

**3-SECOND BIOGRAPHY**
RANDY MOSHER
1952–
Beer evangelist, brewing expert and author of *Tasting Beer*, a comprehensive guide to understanding and appreciating beer

**30-SECOND TEXT**
Sophie Atherton

*Understanding what it is you're tasting can make beer all the more enjoyable.*

# BAR

# STORAGE & SERVICE

## the 30-second beer

**RELATED ENTRIES**
See also
PACKAGING & DISPENSE
page 24

CONDITIONING &
MATURATION
page 52

**3-SECOND TASTER**
The final steps in its journey from brewer to consumer, the cellaring and service of beer, are time-honoured traditions requiring skill and dedication.

**3-MINUTE BREW**
Different beers and ales demand different glassware. Flutes concentrate sparkle and accentuate crispness, while a flared shape allows a voluptuous head to form on top of wheat beers and the like. Pint glasses, dimpled and otherwise, deliver a refreshing draught, but to enjoy the fragrance of a hoppy pilsner or a rich old ale, pour it into a tulip-shaped glass or a brandy balloon and give it a swirl.

Four things matter most when serving beer in the best condition: hygiene, temperature, glassware and the pour. The knowledge and skill of the bartender or publican are what brings it all together. However beer arrives, whether in bottle, can, cask or keg, it's a sensitive soul and needs to be prepared for service. This varies from simply chilling in a fridge to cellaring for weeks until its condition is just right. Beer needs to be stored in a scrupulously clean environment out of sunlight, at a temperature of 8–12°C (46–54°F). Real ale in particular, like fresh food, has a limited lifespan. While opinions do differ, as a rule, lagers should be served between 6°C and 10°C (43 and 50°F), and cask and keg-conditioned ales between 10°C and 14°C (50 and 57°F). Similar guidelines apply to refrigerated beer, with lagers at the lowest temperatures, and barley wines and imperial stouts brought to room temperature before serving – being too cold tends to mute aroma and flavour. The final act, the pour, is equally important. Judging the right angle and the correct speed to deliver the perfect head of foam takes practice. Guinness is not alone in having its own pouring ritual. Wheat beers, pilsners and nitro stouts are among those requiring special attention, while bottle-conditioned beers need care so as to disturb the yeasty sediment as little as possible.

**3-SECOND BIOGRAPHIES**
VACLAV BERKA
1956–
Third-generation brewmaster at Pilsner Urquell; globetrotting advocate of the proper service and enjoyment of good beer

RAY DANIELS
1958–
Craft beer industry veteran who in 2007 founded the Cicerone Certification Program, the training scheme for those buying and serving beer

**30-SECOND TEXT**
Susanna Forbes

*To serve beer in its best condition, treat each style differently, seeking out the right glassware and checking the serving temperature.*

# BEER QUALITY

## the 30-second beer

Whether draught, bottled or canned, beer should pour with a lively head of foam and be crystal clear in the glass – unless it's a style meant to have a haze, such as German wheat beer. The major enemies of good beer are oxygen and light. When draught beer is drawn from its container there's the risk that the carbon dioxide that gives beer its sparkle or 'condition' will be replaced by oxygen from the atmosphere. Packaged beers in bottles or cans that have been poorly sealed or left on shelves for too long also run the risk of becoming oxidized. The result is beer with unpleasant wet paper, cardboard or vegetable flavours. Bottled beers left on shelves under bright lights can become 'light struck', resulting in a stale and salty flavour. A similar fault is created if beer is left in bright sunshine. Another quality issue is over-carbonation, which can give beer a very fizzy character, as well as creating sensations of prickling and burning. It can also make the drinker feel bloated. While cask beer has low, natural carbonation from secondary fermentation in the container, keg beers and lagers are usually filtered and are served by applied $CO_2$. On the other hand, beer that is under-carbonated (or old or stale) will be flat without a head.

**3-SECOND TASTER**
Beer is a cool, delicious drink but things can go wrong if it is exposed to oxygen or bright light, or stored in an unsuitable environment.

**3-MINUTE BREW**
Hygiene is vital when storing and serving beer. Cellars must be kept scrupulously clean and the 'lines' or plastic tubes connected to casks and kegs that take beer to the bar must be washed through regularly. Glasses need to be sparkling, free from detergents and kept cool – beer should never be poured into a warm glass taken from the dishwasher. Glasses that haven't been cleaned properly can also result in flat beer.

**RELATED ENTRY**
See also
STORAGE & SERVICE
page 138

**3-SECOND BIOGRAPHY**
PAUL NUNNY
1949–
Originally a chartered accountant, Nunny went on to work for Adnams Brewery in Suffolk. His experience here enabled him to co-found Cask Marque, a groundbreaking beer quality accreditation scheme to which some 10,000 British pubs are signed up

**30-SECOND TEXT**
Roger Protz

*Beer can be spoiled without proper care and attention, developing a range of undesirable and unpleasant off flavours.*

# BEER & FOOD MATCHING

## the 30-second beer

### 3-SECOND TASTER
Matching beer and food needn't be rocket science; they are perfect partners with many more flavours in common than wine and food.

### 3-MINUTE BREW
A 2003 book by Brooklyn Brewery's Garrett Oliver gave beer and food matching a huge boost. Called *The Brewmaster's Table*, it remains a seminal work. In Europe, most notably Belgium, pairing beer and food is nothing new and it's not unusual to find restaurants suggesting beers to match your meal. The rest of the world is still catching up, but the USA and UK are home to plenty of advocates for the idea.

**Beer is a natural partner to food** and may be a better match for dining than wine. There are many approaches to matching but the simplest is to consider flavour, balance and intensity – FBI for short. Flavours in both beer and food should work together rather than clashing, in a similar way to how ingredients work in a recipe. In terms of balance, neither beer nor food should overwhelm, although a good match may increase the enjoyment of both or emphasize certain aspects of flavour. Intensity refers to the rule of thumb of pairing subtly flavoured beers with simple, lightly seasoned dishes; medium beers with food that shares similar depth of taste, and intense beers with more strongly flavoured foods. It's also a reminder to start subtle and work up to strong flavour if matching several courses. The sheer diversity of flavours, often coming from only four basic ingredients, are key to beer's food pairing versatility, while carbonation is perfect for refreshing and cleansing the palate. Malt naturally echoes many foods from bread and cakes to roasted flavours. Hops have much in common with fruits and spices, but can emphasize spicy heat and bitterness. Yeast can also pose a challenge as it can alter flavours in unexpected ways. The simplest method is experimentation, and taste testing what works, before sharing with others.

### RELATED ENTRIES
See also
BELGIUM
page 96

GARRETT OLIVER
page 144

### 3-SECOND BIOGRAPHIES
MARK DORBER
1957–
Pioneering publican, formerly at one of London's most famous beer specialist pubs: The White Horse, Parsons Green. Early advocate of beer and food matching. Co-founder of beer training organization, The Beer & Cider Academy, which accredits beer sommeliers in the UK

MELISSA COLE
1975–
British beer evangelist and author renowned for her beer and food matching skills and knowledge

### 30-SECOND TEXT
Sophie Atherton

*The right beer and food pairing can make both even more enjoyable, a bit like having good company at the dining table.*

**29 JULY 1962**
Born in Queens, New York

**1981**
Studies broadcasting and film at Boston University

**1983**
Becomes stage manager, University of London Union

**1989**
Becomes apprentice brewer, Manhattan Brewing Company, then brewmaster in 1993

**1994**
Joins Brooklyn Brewery; oversees building of brewhouse, which opens in 1996

**1997**
First modern brewing collaboration between Brooklyn Brewery and Brakspears Brewery, Henley-on-Thames, England

**1998**
Receives Russell Schehrer Award for Innovation and Excellence in Brewing from Institute for Brewing Studies, the USA's highest brewing accolade

**2003**
Publishes *The Brewmaster's Table*

**2011**
Publishes *The Oxford Companion to Beer*

**2012**
Made an Honorary Beer Sommelier by The Institute of Brewing & Distilling

**2014**
Receives James Beard Foundation Award for Outstanding Wine, Beer or Spirits Professional

**2014**
Establishes New Carnegie Brewery with Carlsberg in Stockholm, first of global network of partnerships

**2014**
Launches The Art & Science of Brewing at Culinary Institute of America

**2016**
Releases The Serpent, a groundbreaking collaboration between Brooklyn, Thornbridge Brewery and Oliver's Cider & Perry

# GARRETT OLIVER

'The brewmaster is more like a chef than he is like a winemaker', wrote Garrett Oliver in *The Brewmaster's Table*. With trademark clarity, Oliver, brewmaster at Brooklyn Brewery since 1994, set the scene for the cultural feast that was to follow.

Already one of America's most influential brewers, with the publication of *The Brewmaster's Table* in 2003, Oliver became pivotal in reshaping the world's appreciation of beer. Michael Jackson had begun the food pairing discourse 10 years earlier in *The Beer Companion*. With Oliver, it came of age. Beers come to life on the page in *The Brewmaster's Table*. The people appear centre-stage. And the food matches draw on the widest possible range of cuisines. All those involved with beer and gastronomy drew inspiration to enjoy and explore further, as the book's subtitle sums up, 'the pleasures of real beer with real food'.

Oliver grew up in a happy Queens household in New York and was often to be found experimenting in the kitchen at weekends. Good beer, however, didn't arrive until his early twenties. Encountering his first pint of 'real ale' the day he landed in England, Oliver spent the next year exploring this new vista amid the London pub scene. Next came Europe, where Oliver avidly immersed himself in the local cuisines and cultures. Frustrated with the quality of beer upon his return to New York, Oliver took up homebrewing. While president of the New York Homebrewers' Guild he met Steve Hindy, soon-to-be co-founder with Tom Potter of Brooklyn Brewery.

Oliver joined the Manhattan Brewery in 1989, swiftly making his mark. He came to the attention of Michael Jackson, who introduced him to the Great American Beer Festival. In 1994 Oliver crossed the river to join Hindy and Potter at Brooklyn Brewery. With typical flair, his 'application' for the brewmaster post was a showstopping beer: what became Brooklyn's Black Chocolate Stout. *The Brewmaster's Table* was followed, eight years later, by *The Oxford Companion to Beer*, the ultimate reference work. Back in the brewhouse, Oliver continues to innovate. Among the first to explore secondary bottle fermentation in detail, his barrel ageing programme has also grown in stature, now encompassing over 2,000 barrels.

Oliver has helped Brooklyn Brewery to forge partnerships around the world, and is particularly proud of the link-up with America's top cooking school, the Culinary Institute of America. Along the way, he's hosted over 1,000 dinners in over 20 countries, plus numerous television appearances, from the History Channel to *The Martha Stewart Show*. All in a day's work for this renaissance man.

*Susanna Forbes*

# BEER WRITING

## the 30-second beer

Why write about beer? That is, why write about its flavour or the culture of beer rather than just about how to make it or where to drink some? Because beer is the world's most popular alcoholic beverage, staggeringly varied, and so, inherently interesting. And, because not everybody knows this, its stories need to be told. Maybe UK journalist Michael Jackson thought something like this when he started writing about beer as a sideline to his day job. In his 1977 book *The World Guide to Beer*, Jackson used language reminiscent of wine tasting and effectively invented the concept of beer styles. And with Tim Webb separately expounding Belgium's myriad but almost forgotten beers, there emerged a desire to emulate these beers in the USA. Descriptive writing about beer and its culture took off and gave us beer journalists, guilds of beer writers in North America and Britain, print and online specialist magazines, beer columns in mainstream newspapers and books of all descriptions – some even involving matching beer and food. The internet meant the amateur could contribute, spawning waves of beer blogs, then podcasts. Beer-rating sites soon followed. RateBeer.com's success attracted investment from brewing giant AB InBev. Four decades on, and various world guides later, there are still many beer stories to be told.

**RELATED ENTRIES**
See also
BELGIUM
page 96

MICHAEL JACKSON
page 102

UNITED STATES
page 104

**3-SECOND TASTER**
The other Michael Jackson revealed world beers, invented modern beer writing and inspired America to re-invent beer – now people rate their pint on social media.

**3-MINUTE BREW**
As important as books are to beer writing, magazines like *All About Beer* in the USA, *C/O Hops* in Sweden and *Beer and Brewer* in Australia and New Zealand provided outlets for beer enthusiasts to get into print. The internet has made beer writing a truly worldwide phenomenon; you can now read about beer from everywhere anywhere.

**3-SECOND BIOGRAPHIES**
JEAN DE CLERK
1902–78
Belgian brewing technician and author of technical books about beer that led Michael Jackson to think about organizing different beer types as styles

STAN HIERONYMUS
1948–
American beer journalist and amateur brewer. Went full time as a beer writer in 1993. Editor of www.realbeer.com and writes the blog appellationbeer. com. Author of many books about brewing and craft beer

**30-SECOND TEXT**
Jerry Bartlett

*The best beer writing is inclusive, informative and inspiring.*

# BEER JUDGING

## the 30-second beer

**RELATED ENTRY**
See also
HOW TO TASTE BEER
page 136

**3-SECOND BIOGRAPHY**
PATRICK BAKER
1936–
Co-founder, with Charlie Papazian, of the Beer Judge Certification Program in 1985, with the aim of giving beer judging more credibility

**30-SECOND TEXT**
Jeff Evans

**3-SECOND TASTER**
Judging takes beer appreciation to a new level. Competitions demand that every aspect of a beer is scrutinized in order to find the very best.

**3-MINUTE BREW**
Anyone considering becoming a beer judge can find out more by taking a dedicated beer judging course. The longest established is the Beer Judge Certification Program (BJCP), which, although based in the USA, now offers courses in other countries, too. In the UK, the Beer & Cider Academy runs its own 'How to Judge Beer' course. Both courses offer examinations leading to a certificate.

Judging beer can be great fun and a fascinating learning experience. It's a process that takes knowledge acquired through tasting beer for pleasure and places it in a formal context, challenging you to think deeply about the products in front of you and balancing your views with those of other informed people. The process involves evaluating beers on the basis of appearance, aroma, taste and finish, but also, quite often, on how closely they conform to precise styles of beer. Judges work as part of a team and there can be heated discussions before the winner is decided. Some competitions are exclusively judged by brewers or other experts. Others, such as local CAMRA events in the UK or homebrew competitions in the USA, allow participation by amateur enthusiasts. The major beer competition in the USA is held as part of the Great American Beer Festival, echoing the Champion Beer of Britain contest organized by CAMRA in the UK. Many countries or continents now have their own equivalents, such as Birra dell'Anno in Italy and Copa Latinoamericana de Cervezas Artesanales in South America. Globally, there are a number of influential competitions that cross national boundaries, including the World Beer Cup, the International Brewing Awards, the International Beer Challenge, the European Beer Star, the World Beer Awards and the Brussels Beer Challenge.

*The best competitions are 'blind tastings', with beer only identified by a number, so judges don't know which beer they are judging.*

# BEER FESTIVALS

## the 30-second beer

There is no greater celebration of beer than Munich's Oktoberfest. This annual party is based around 14 huge beer tents run by the city's breweries. It is a grand-scale example of many similar cultural events that involve beer around the world, from the humble village fete to sizzling summer barbecues. Events focused more precisely on beer began in the 1970s in the UK, where the Campaign for Real Ale (CAMRA) was looking to draw attention to traditional ales that were disappearing from British pubs. It found the answer in running its own temporary 'pubs', using town halls or marquees to present a huge selection of beers that would impress the drinking public. CAMRA still runs dozens of beer festivals, with the pinnacle the Great British Beer Festival in London. This was the template for the Great American Beer Festival, staged in Denver every autumn, and many other events around the world, such as Mondial de la Bière in Canada and Beertopia in Hong Kong. At beer festivals, the public either pays a modest entrance fee and then buys beers as they would in a bar or pays a higher entrance fee and receives free beers as small samples. Both systems enable drinkers to sample a vast array of beers, while also enjoying live music, talks and other entertainment.

**RELATED ENTRIES**
See also
BEER IN THE TWENTIETH CENTURY
page 42

BEER CHAMPIONS
page 152

**3-SECOND TASTER**
Beer festivals provide wonderful opportunities to sample an amazing selection of beers of varying styles, from breweries big and small.

**3-MINUTE BREW**
The Great British Beer Festival, first held in 1977, offers more than 900 beers and attracts more than 40,000 visitors over five days every August. The first Great American Beer Festival was staged in 1982. Just 24 breweries participated, pouring 47 beers, but 800 people showed up, encouraging the American Homebrewers Association, which ran it, to try again the following year. Today, it attracts 800 breweries and some 60,000 attendees over its three-day run.

**3-SECOND BIOGRAPHY**
CROWN PRINCE LUDWIG
1786–1868
The future King Ludwig I of Bavaria whose marriage to Princess Therese of Saxony-Hildburghausen on 12 October 1810 was celebrated with a public party that later developed into the Oktoberfest – the mother of all beer festivals

**30-SECOND TEXT**
Jeff Evans

*Beer festivals provide a wonderful opportunity to celebrate and sample a wide range of brews available in one place.*

# BEER CHAMPIONS

## the 30-second beer

The best known and most influential champion of beer is the British Campaign for Real Ale – CAMRA for short. It was founded in 1971 after a series of mergers and takeovers created six large national brewers. They were determined to phase out cask ale and replace it with sweet, gassy and artificially carbonated keg beer. The campaign grew quickly, publishing a monthly newspaper, *What's Brewing*, and the annual *Good Beer Guide* listing all known pubs serving cask beer. Today it has close to 200,000 members and runs beer festivals throughout the UK, featuring beer from independent brewers. CAMRA joined forces with European counterparts in 1990 to form the European Beer Consumers Union (EBCU). The most influential groups were the Objectieve Bierproevers in Belgium – now called Zythos – and PINT in the Netherlands. Members campaign to preserve regional and local beer traditions, support independent breweries and resist attempts to homogenize beer and reduce its diversity and variety. Today there are member organizations in Austria, the Czech Republic, Denmark, Finland, France, Ireland, Italy, the Netherlands, Norway, Poland, Spain, Sweden and Switzerland. CAMRA also has a sister organization in North America, CAMRA Canada.

## RELATED ENTRIES
See also
PACKAGING & DISPENSE
page 24

MICHAEL JACKSON
page 102

GARRETT OLIVER
page 144

BEER WRITING
page 146

## 3-SECOND BIOGRAPHIES
MICHAEL HARDMAN
1946–
Co-founded CAMRA. Former editor of *Good Beer Guide* and *What's Brewing*. Also co-founded the British Guild of Beer Writers

CONRAD SEIDL
1958–
Known as the *Bierpapst* or Beer Pope, he writes extensively about Austrian and German beer in the daily newspaper *Der Standard*

## 30-SECOND TEXT
Roger Protz

*Beer champions make it their mission to tell the world about their favourite drink.*

### 3-SECOND TASTER
Beer might be a lot less amazing without champions to defend and promote it – probably the most successful example is the UK's Campaign for Real Ale.

### 3-MINUTE BREW
Beer's popularity is cause for celebration and concern. Some value it for the brewer's skill in creating a wide variety of drinks from just four ingredients; others see it merely as a money maker. Beer champions tend to hold the former view, although that doesn't mean they think brewing shouldn't be a business! Beer champions are needed whenever beer quality and diversity is threatened by putting profit ahead of good beer. Other modern threats include rising taxation and the anti-alcohol lobby.

## RESOURCES

### BOOKS

*The Beer & Food Companion*
Stephen Beaumont
(Jacqui Small, 2015)

*Brew Britannia*
Jessica Boak & Ray Bailey
(Aurum Press, 2014)

*The Brewmaster's Table*
Garrett Oliver
(HarperCollins, 2003)

*Let Me Tell You About Beer*
Melissa Cole
(Pavilion, 2011)

*Michael Jackson's Beer Companion*
Michael Jackson
(Mitchell Beazley, 1993)

*The Oxford Companion to Beer*
Garrett Oliver
(Oxford University Press, 2011)

*The Perfect Pint*
Andy Hamilton
(Bantam Press, 2018)

*Tasting Beer*
Randy Mosher
(Storey Publishing, 2009)

*The World Atlas of Beer*
Tim Webb and Stephen Beaumont
(Mitchell Beazley, 2016)

*The World Guide to Beer*
Michael Jackson
(Mitchell Beazley, 1979)

### WEBSITES

The Beer Advocate
US-based website founded in 1996 by Jason
and Todd Alström, who went on to found a
magazine of the same name. Great reads and
resources on all aspects of beer.
www.beeradvocate.com

British Hop Association
Information and explanation about the
UK's hops and growers, and its famed
hop-breeding programme.
www.britishhops.org.uk

CraftBeer.com
From the US Brewers Association, bringing news
and information.
www.craftbeer.com

## EVENTS

Borefts Beer Festival
Small, exclusive annual two-day festival
held late September by Brouwerij de Molen,
in Bodegraven (about 40km (25 miles)
southwest of Amsterdam) in the Netherlands.
brouwerijdemolen.nl/en/borefts-beerfestival/

The Great American Beer Festival
Annual beer extravaganza held each
October in Denver, Colorado by the
Brewers Association.
www.greatamericanbeerfestival.com

The Great British Beer Festival
CAMRA's legendary annual festival at
London Olympia.
www.gbbf.org.uk

Indy Man Beer Con
The cool kids of the brewing world head to
Manchester; held in the iconic Victoria Baths.
www.indymanbeercon.co.uk

Oktoberfest
Held in Munich, this is the world's biggest
beer celebration.
www.oktoberfest.de/en/

## RETAILERS

The Bottle Shop
Based in the south-east of England, The Bottle
Shop started life as a stall selling craft beer, to
take away or drink on site, at an indoor farmers'
market in Canterbury; now has bars in Margate
and London, as well as an online shop and a
wholesale arm.
bottle.shop

Eebria
Web platform and storefront, from which
you can order from some of the UK's leading
breweries.
www.eebria.com

Utobeer/The Cage
Long established beer merchants in
London's Borough Market, owned by two
extremely knowledgeable and passionate
beer pioneers, also behind tiny nearby bar
and beer institution, The Rake.
boroughmarket.org.uk/traders/utobeer

# NOTES ON CONTRIBUTORS

### EDITOR

**Sophie Atherton** is a writer and journalist, and was the first woman in the UK to be accredited as a beer sommelier. Her work appears regularly in the UK national press and various magazines such as the Campaign for Real Ale's *BEER* and trade publication *The Morning Advertiser*, in which she writes a monthly column. She is an accomplished beer judge in both the UK and USA, at competitions including the World Beer Cup, International Beer Challenge, SIBA National Beer Competition and CAMRA's Champion Beer of Britain. As well as being a beer writer she is also a consultant and PR adviser with clients throughout the beer and pub industry. www.afemaleview.net

### FOREWORD

**Roger Ryman** has 30 years' experience in the brewing industry and has spent around 20 of those at St Austell Brewery, Cornwall. In 2016 he took over the reins of newly acquired Bath Ales and now oversees beer production and both brewery sites. Qualified with an MSc in Brewing and Distilling Science from Heriot-Watt University, he also holds the Master Brewer qualification of the Institute of Brewing and Distilling and was recently made a Fellow of the same. He has been recognized as a Brewer of the Year by both the British Guild of Beer Writers and the All-Party Parliamentary Beer Group and is also a Freeman of the City of London and a Liveryman of the Company of Brewers, an ancient guild of brewers dating from the fifteenth century.

### CONTRIBUTORS

**Jerry Bartlett** is a freelance writer and Swedophile. He has been writing about beer, whisky and food as MaltJerry since 2010, winning an award for Online Communication from the British Guild of Beer Writers the same year. Jerry is also a beer and whisky judge, counting 15 years at the Stockholm Beer and Whisky festival; twice with legendary 'Beer Hunter/Whisky Chaser' Michael Jackson, and the International Beer Challenge. www.maltjerry.com.

**Pete Brown** is a British writer who specializes in making people thirsty. He is the author of eight books and writes numerous articles in the drinks trade press and consumer press. He appears regularly on TV and radio, and has judged competitions including the BBC Food and Farming Awards and Great Taste Awards. He's a member of the British Guild of Beer Writers, and was named Beer Writer of the Year in 2009, 2012 and 2016.

**Jeff Evans** has been writing professionally about beer for 30 years. He is a former editor of CAMRA's *Good Beer Guide* and author of many acclaimed books, including *A Beer a Day*, *The Book of Beer Knowledge*, the *Good Bottled Beer Guide* and *So You Want to Be a Beer Expert*? A former UK Beer Writer of the Year, he gives talks, hosts tastings and broadcasts about beer and is chairman of the judges for the International Beer Challenge. www.insidebeer.com

**Susanna Forbes** is a freelance writer, editorial consultant and events organizer, with 20 years' experience in the drinks trade. Beer and cider editor of *Imbibe* and *Imbibe Live*, she specializes in pubs, bars and restaurants, champions beer and food matching, and is a regular beer judge. A firm advocate of meeting the people behind the pint, she set up DrinkBritain.com, the drinks tourism website. With her husband she recently founded Little Pomona Orchard & Cidery.

**Roger Protz** is a beer writer with a worldwide reputation. He has written more than 20 books and edited 24 editions of the annual *Good Beer Guide*. He has won gold and silver awards from the British and American Guilds of Beer Writers and has twice won the Glenfiddich Drink Writer of the Year award. He has lectured to Friends of the Smithsonian Museum in Washington DC and Beer Expo in Melbourne, Australia. He judges in many international competitions, including the Brussels Beer Challenge. He has been given Lifetime Achievement Awards by the British Guild of Beer Writers and the Society of Independent Brewers and has been named an Honorary Knight by the Belgian Brewers' Federation. www.protzonbeer.co.uk

# INDEX

# ACKNOWLEDGEMENTS

EDITOR'S ACKNOWLEDGMENTS
I would like to thank my husband (aka 'Beer Husband'), Nick Claxton, for his help and support while writing and editing *30-Second Beer*.

PICTURE CREDITS
The publisher would like to thank the following for permission to reproduce copyright material on the following pages:

Alamy /INTERFOTO: 97BL; /Paul Fearn: 31C, 37BR, 38; /still light: 73C (b/ground); /Ville Palonen: 109C; /WENN Ltd: 144.
Bavarian State Painting Collections/Neue Pinakothek Munich 11CR, 151CR.
Biodiversity Heritage Library. Digitized by Harvard University Botany Libraries 7TL, 7TR, 7TC, 7CL, 7CR, 7BL, 7BR, 51CL, 55TL, 55TR, 55TC, 55CL, 55CR, 55BL, 55BR.
Brewdog 128.
CAMRA 121C, 153TC, 153BC.
Clip Art 25BC, 53B, 121BL, 121BR, 147BC.
Dr Peter Darby, Wye Hops Ltd 56.
Library of Congress, Washington, D.C. 77CL, 77CR, 87TR (John Margolies Roadside America photograph archive), 87CL (National Photo Company Collection), 99BR, 99CR, 105BR (U.S. Farm Security Administration/Office of War Information), 125T, 127CR, 147TL, 147TCR, 147BR.
Mikkeller 107T, 107CR.
Nationaal Archief, Netherlands /Joop van Bilsen/Anefo: 103T.
Omnipollo 107BL, 107BC, 107BR.
PublicDomainPictures.net /George Hodan 99CR; /Karen Arnold: 95CL.
Rijksmuseum, Netherlands 61BR.
Jeff Scott/beergeek.com 102.
Shutterstock /Africa Studio: 17TC, 139C, 149BC; /Aha-Soft: 49TC; /Alesia Hsiao: 109TR; /Aleynikov Pavel: 87BC; /Anastasiika: 37TR; /Andras Szen: 137T; /Andrii Horulko: 75TC; /Andris Tkacenko: 75TC; /Anna Kucherova: 85BC; /annalisa e marina durante: 21BR; /Anton Ivanov: 73BC, 119B; /antoni halim: 33TC; /Anucha Tiemsom: 2CL, 65CL, 75TC, 75C; /aquariagirl1970: 131CL; /AVA Bitter: 59CL; /ayzek: 109TR; /Babich Alexander: 21BR; /Bart Sadowski: 121T; /belkos: 149TC; /Bikeworldtravel: 25TR; /Boris-B: 99T; /Boule: 131C; /Bozena: 2CR, 65CR; /By Hard Ligth: 143T; /chippix: 89TC, 125B, 131C; /Chones: 21TL; /Christopher Hall: 51BC, 51BR; /Claudio Divizia: 49CR; /clearviewstock: 33C (b/ground); /Coprid: 35BR; /COZ: 75BL; /CSD Dmitriy Tikhonenko: 25TL; /Danny Smythe: 2BL, 65BL; /Darla Hallmark: 63B (b/ground); /Deidra McKenzie: 85T; /DenisMArt: 41TL, 105CR; /Digital Media Pro: 87TC; /dikobraziy: 111TL; /Dionisvera: 2C, 65C; /Dja65: 25BL; /Dmitri_st: 141CL; /dny3d: 11TC, 151TC; /Dmitry Naumov: 63BC, 75BR, 103C, 139TR, 143CR; /DutchScenery: 9TL, 9TR, 9BR, 19TR, 19TL, 19BR 51C; /Elena Sherengovskaya: 83B (b/ground); /Epine: 17TC, 17BC; /Everett – Art: 97CR; /Everett Collection: 113CL, 113CR, 125B, 153TCR, 153TCL; /Everett Historical: 2C, 10BC, 11CL, 17CR, 17CL, 31B, 33BCL, 33BCR, 33B, 43C, 43BR, 59TC; 63BR; 65C; 73TC, 137BC, 151CL, 123 (upper row); /Fascinadora: 51BR, 51BL, 61BR; /Feel good studio: 83C; /FooT Too: 131CBR; /Forest Foxy: 147TCL; /fotomak: 109TL; /Frank11: 77TC; /Frantisekf: 41BC; /freeskyline: 11BC; 151BC; /FXQuadro: 121TC; /Georgios Kollidas: 41TR; /Gor Grigoryan: 17TC; /green_01: 83TR; /Gregory Gerber: 143C; /Gwoeii: 111CL; /Hein Nouwens: 41BL, 65TR, 113TC, 143CL, 153B; HiSunnySky: 7BC, 55BC; /icosha: 109CR; /Igor Iakovlev: 139BC; /Irina Danyliuk: 11TC, 151TC; /Iterum: 35C (b/ground); /Ivan Kulikov: 9BL, 9BR, 19BL, 19BR; /Ivan Smuk: 77 (b/ground); /Ivonne Wierink: 153TR, 153TL; /jaap posthumus: 149CL; /Jane Rix: 137C; /Jaroslaw Grudzinski: 85BR; /JHK2303: 71TC; /Joe Gough: 143CR; /Joshua Rainey: 49CR, 87CL; /jsp: 31C (b/ground); /kc look: 143BC; /Ken StockPhoto: 127T; /Kev Gregory: 149BR, 149CR; /Kichigin: 75T (b/ground); /Kirill Z: 59CR, 143CL; /Kishivan: 25BR; /Knorre: 61T; /Kovaleva_Ka: 89TL; /Kubko: 119B; /KUCO: 89TC, 143C; /Kyselova Inna: 75TC; /LALS STOCK: 59BR; /Lev Kropotov: 113CR; /Lightspring: 113TL; /LiliGraphie: 95BR; /LUMIKK555: 99R; /Luciano Mortula – LGM: 105C; /LunaseeStudios: 105BL; /Macrovector: 113BL, 113BR; /Madlen: 97CL, 97CR; /Maks: 2CL, 65C; /Maks Narodenko: 105T; /Mariyana M: 141C; /mart: 35T; /Marzolino: 37C, 71BC, 77C; /MaxyM: 10BR; 137BR; /Meilun: 37TL; /melis: 149C (b/ground); /Mikhail Pogosov: 63C; /Mile Atanasov: 139C; /mitchinovphotograph: 41CR; /Morphart Creation: 41CR, 49CL, 81TL, 107B (b/ground), 123TL, 123BC; /Mtsaride: 71BC; /NaMaKuKi: 89B; /Nata Alhontess: 17BL, 17BR, 121TCL, 121TCR; /Nataliya Hora: 49CL; /Nataly Reinch: 109BL; /nazlisart: 105TR; /Nejron Photo: 111TCR; /Nerthuz: 49CR, 131CL; /nevodka: 131CR; /niceregionpics: 111TR; /oculo: 147TC; /OkFoto: 113CR; /Olga Popova: 43TR; /Osipovfoto: 113TC; /osoznanie.jizni: 7C, 55C; /paulista: 83BR, 139TL, 139TR; /Peter Gudella: 85B, 143B (b/ground); /photocritical: 131T (b/ground); /Photo Melon: 149BC, 149TR; /photo one: 63TL; /plustkon: 141CL; /Pocholo Calapre: 107T; /populustremula: 81BR; /PRESSLAB: 53TL; /Quayside: 99CR; /railway fx: 109TL, 113CL; /rawf8: 139B; /r.classen: 75BCL, 139TL, 139TC; /RedDaxLuma: 123TC; /Red monkey: 113BC (b/ground); /Remitski Ivan: 53BC; /Richard Thornton: 87C; /ricochet64: 147TL; /Rob Wilson: 105BL; /Roger Siljander: 21CR, 123TR, 123BR, 123BL; /sacilad: 22; /sagir: 99BR; /Sapnocte: 53BL; /Sergiy Kuzmin: 37TC, 37BR; /Sirisak Chantorn: 49BR; /siro46: 35BR, 43TL; /sirtravelalot: 63CR; /somchaij: 75BCL; /SOMMAI 2CR, 65CR, 141B; /spinetta: 147BL; /SP-Photo: 11TL, 11TR, 151TL, 151TR; /Steve Cukrov: 105BR, 111BC; /stockphoto-graf: 99CL; /Stocksnapper: 61BR; /Stoker-13: 97C (b/ground); /Stone36: 2BR, 65R; /Stuart Monk: 75TC; /StudioPhotoDFlorez: 75TC, 75CL, 75C, 75CR; /sunabesyou: 111CR; /Susan Law Cain: 1123 (bottom row); /Tanya_mtv: 85CR; /Tatiana Kasyanova: 147CL; /Tatiana Volgutova: 95BR; /Tatyana Prikhodko: 75TC, 75CL, 75C, 75CR; /thefoodphotographer: 97CR; /ThiagoSantos: 59BR; /Thumbelina: 31BC; /Tim UR: 2C, 65C, 83B, 85BC; /TKalinowski: 81BC; /toeytoey: 51TC; /topseller: 89TR; /Valentina Razumova: 7TC, 7CL, 7CR, 55TC, 55CL, 55CR; /Valentyn Volkov: 53CL, 77BR, 85BL; /Vectorcarrot: 49TC; /Vectorgoods studio: 2BC, 65BC, 85BC; /Victor Maschek: 103C (b/ground); /vixenkristy: 9CL, 9CR, 19CL, 19CR; /vnlit: 89T; /WEB-DESIGN: 17TC; /You Touch Pix of EuToch: 95T; /yuttana Contributor Studio: 49C; /Zovteva: 143C, 149CR; /Zvonimir Atletic: 33C; /zydesign: 97TR.
Stichting Academisch Erfgoedl 51CR.
U.S. Department of Agriculture Pomological Watercolor Collection 51CL.
Wellcome Collection (CC BY 4.0) 33BL, 35TR, 51BC.
Wikimedia Commons 41CL, 78.

All reasonable efforts have been made to trace copyright holders and to obtain their permission for the use of copyright material. The publisher apologizes for any errors or omissions in the list above and will gratefully incorporate any corrections in future reprints if notified.